BEAT JET LAG

Arrive Alert and Stay Alert

Kathleen Mayes

Thorsons
An Imprint of HarperCollins*Publishers*

Thorsons
An Imprint of GraftonBooks
A Division of HarperCollins*Publishers*
77-85 Fulham Palace Road,
Hammersmith, London W6 8JB

Published by Thorsons 1991

1   3   5   7   9   10   8   6   4   2

British Library Cataloguing in Publication Data
Mayes, Kathleen
Beat jet lag.
1. Air travel. Medical aspects
I. Title
613.68

ISBN 0 7225 2343 2

Typeset by Harper Phototypesetters Limited,
Northampton, England
Printed in Great Britain by
HarperCollinsManufacturing, Glasgow

'Our body is a well-set clock, which keeps good time, but if it be too much or indiscreetly tampered with, the alarm runs out before the hour.'

—Joseph Hall, Bishop of Norwich, 1574-1656

'. . . the direct interpretation of space and time by means of measuring rods and clocks, now breaks down . . .'

—Albert Einstein, 1935

CONTENTS

NOTE TO THE READER

No responsibility is assumed on the part of the author, the publisher, or the distributors of this work. It is not the purpose of this publication to replace the services of a physician, nor is it the purpose to guarantee any medicinal or nutritional preparation or the effectiveness thereof.

This information is presented not with the intention of diagnosing or prescribing. Before beginning any change in diet or exercise, it is recommended that you should consult your doctor. If you are on a special diet under the direction of your doctor or health professional, consult him or her before using the programmes and exercises mentioned in this guide. It is important to follow your doctor's instructions.

Any use of brand names in this guide is for identification only, and does not imply endorsement or otherwise by the author.

Any references to biological rhythms in this book should not be confused with the theory of 'biorhythms'.

ACKNOWLEDGEMENTS

This guide is based on far more than personal experience of jet-lag problems and their solutions. Many people have contributed their time, advice and material for the preparation of this book. I want to express my thanks not only to my husband, Dorin, for the illustrations, and to Brian J. Blackie, Ph.C., M.P.S., Colin Doran and William Hall for providing reference material, but also to the following organizations for their guidance and encouragement:

Air New Zealand, American Biosearch, Inc., American Sleep Disorders Association, Argonne National Laboratory, Better Sleep Council, Inc., The Boeing Company, British Airways, General Chronobionics, Imperial Chemical Industries plc, International Civil Aviation Organization, Lighting Research Institute, Rockwell International Corporation, Shell Oil Company, The Upjohn Company.

International Time Zones

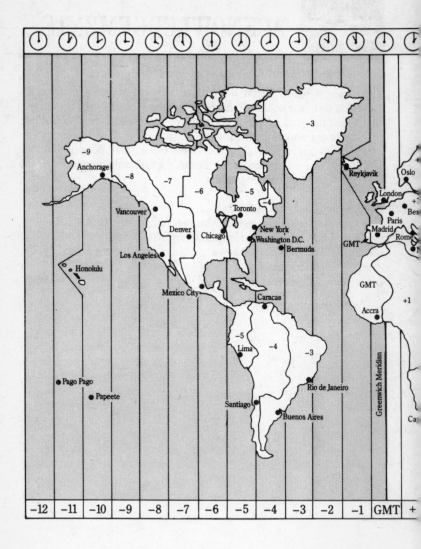

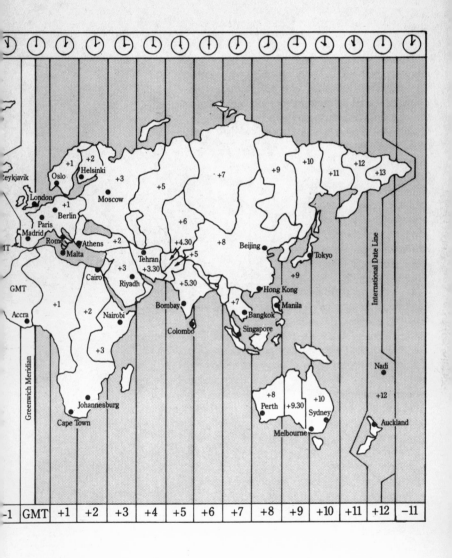

CHAPTER 1 — WHAT IS JET LAG?

Going 'around the world in eighty days' now seems absurd and outdated. No one has the time. Instead, thousands of people are boarding jetliners every minute of the day and thousands of others are just landing. This ebb and flow of passengers and planes goes on around the clock, around the globe, between major airports—Heathrow, Charles de Gaulle, Narita, JFK, LAX and hundreds of others. In the year 2000, the world's airlines will carry an estimated 2000 million passengers.

At the flash of a boarding pass, we are now lifted effortlessly above the clouds to see vast continents and shimmering seas passing below. Business is global. Sports are global. Holidays are global. Colourful brochures cram your travel agent's office, tempting you with holidays in exotic places far from phones and fax, 'getting away from it all' to remote tropical beaches for sizzling in the sun; or airlines offer cheap fares for visits to cousin Vera in New Zealand. The sun never sets on the tourist empire. But travel pictures, business contracts and sports programmes don't tell the full story: getting there may be no fun at all. Aircraft perform flawlessly, but what happens to passengers, flight crews and cabin staff? Jet lag. A mass phenomenon, almost as universal as the common cold.

Travelling in the Space Age equipped with bodies that evolved for living in the Stone Age defies nature. Nothing in our evolutionary history has prepared us for such dislocation. Before the advent of air travel, the movement of humans about the Earth was slow enough that body systems were easily able to cope with time-zone changes. By the time travellers reached their destinations, body clocks had had time to adjust and adaptation occurred unnoticed. The Wright brothers put an end to that luxury.

Whether it's a commercial airliner, the Concorde, a military aircraft, the company plane or private jet, technology lets us leapfrog over time zones, but our biology brings us back to Earth. Some travellers 'fly through the air with the greatest of ease', but for millions each year jet lag is annoying and disruptive, interfering with alertness at business meetings, reducing performance of competitors at top international athletic events, and detracting from holiday pleasure. The symptoms can be uncomfortable, unpleasant and serious. Although no one has ever heard of a traveller actually dying of jet lag *per se,* many passengers suffer so much malaise that they 'want to die'. Frequent fliers can't forget that the word 'travel' comes from the French *'travailler'* —to work hard—and one of the most arduous aspects of travel is jet lag. The body does indeed work hard to adjust its inner biological rhythms and clock mechanisms, making no distinction between the diplomat or film star in first class and the holidaymaker confined to economy. As soon as you arrive at your destination, step out of the aircraft and reset your wrist-watch, you're an 'old-timer': not only is the biochemical system of your body still left running on a different time to the world around you, but your inner mechanisms are out of synchrony with each other.

Within a few hours, you can take off from an airport at sea level and land at another on a mountain top at an altitude of several thousand feet; you can radically alter your climate from near-polar to tropical; or you can fly transmeridionally, across several time zones, in a race with the sun. All these changes in geography bring biological changes in travellers and the need to adapt. How you adapt after a long-haul flight depends on several factors: your age, condition of health, and personal tolerance, how you and your body respond, and whether you are crossing time zones.

What jet lag is not

Jet travel is undeniably fatiguing, especially if you have had last-minute pressures and anxieties, lugging suitcases, tangling in traffic jams, and contending with queues and crowds at airports. But jet lag is *not* caused by travel fatigue—which can have its own cluster of problems such as stress, anxieties and depression. It is *not* caused by travelling at extremely high altitude or high speed, and it is *not* connected with inflight symptoms of motion sickness, ear-popping, or light-headedness from dehydration. It is *not* connected with the fear of flying: the pounding heart, clammy hands and white knuckles at take-off, or the nausea, vomiting or diarrhoea and frequent urination. It is *not* caused by crossing the Equator or the Date Line.

What is jet lag?

It is the group of problems connected with transmeridian flights, and is more properly called *circadian desynchronization* or *circadian dysrhythmia.*

Circadian dysrhythmia usually starts as soon as the jet plane lands at your destination, putting you suddenly in another time zone. Dysrhythmia begins when you have adjusted your wrist-watch to local time but your internal biological clocks are telling you something else. Your inner body clocks have a lingering memory of the rhythms you left behind at home, and want to cling to familiar routines. They resist the changeover to the surroundings at your destination point.

Fortunately, circadian dysrhythmia is only a temporary condition (except for flight crews and cabin staff) until daily cycles and patterns shift to be in harmony with the new time zone and in harmony with each other.

What are the main symptoms?

Daytime sleepiness

The most common problem caused by jet lag is disturbance of your awareness of day/night and your normal wake/sleep patterns. Ninety per cent of travellers say they are bothered by daytime fatigue and sleepiness: an overwhelming, crushing sense of fatigue that makes eyes burn and eyelids heavy; daytime drowsiness that disrupts your work, makes you fall asleep at meetings, affecting your performance (both physical and mental) whether you are an athlete competing at an international event, a diplomat attending a summit meeting, or an executive chairing a high-powered conference. If you yield to the compelling urge to sleep during daylight hours at your new destination, then wake up in the afternoon, you may not be tired enough at bedtime to be able to sleep, which will aggravate insomnia. This symptom can last from two to seven days after a trip, and in extreme cases can drag on for a fortnight or even a month.

Insomnia

Many travellers crossing several time zones complain that they are unable to sleep at night; they have fitful sleep, less deep sleep and dream sleep. Some find that insomnia (referred to by sleep researchers as *transient* insomnia) is extremely disturbing, thus increasing the problem of daytime sleepiness. The symptoms of night-time insomnia and daytime drowsiness last longer than other jet-lag woes, and can be serious because they compound other troubles.

Disorientation

You cannot remember where you are; you feel confused and bewildered, whether walking along the street or awake in the middle of the night.

Poor concentration

Impaired concentration can be especially critical for the businessman or diplomat. Scientists say that severe jet lag causes temporary amnesia: you are unable to focus your attention properly on anything, you cannot think clearly, your memory is muddled, you cannot remember what you should be doing, and cannot write reports because of poor memory and judgement.

In the 1950s, when US Secretary of State John Foster Dulles flew to Egypt to negotiate, immediately upon arrival, for the construction of the Aswan Dam, he later admitted that he had made faulty decisions, and lost the project to the Soviets partly because jet travel had made him so weary and impaired his judgement. Mental alertness may take two days or up to a fortnight to adjust.

Slower reflexes

This symptom disturbs two-thirds of jet travellers. It creates hazards if, for example, you are trying to cross streets where traffic comes from an unaccustomed direction, such as the left instead of the right. Slower response time, coupled with impairment of fast visual focusing, reduced night vision and diminished peripheral vision, can cause problems if you are driving in a strange city immediately after landing.

Even superbly-conditioned athletes can be affected. Some years ago, when diver Greg Louganis was at Olympic trials in Moscow, he reported that he had struck his head on a diving platform because jet lag had impaired his coordination. Your coordination and reflexes can take five to ten days to return to normal.

Indigestion

Up to 50 per cent of long-distance passengers say that jet travel alters their digestion (quite apart from digestive upsets that may be caused by eating too quickly, drinking and eating too much, or coping with unfamiliar foods and contaminated water in a foreign country). Jet lag can give you poor appetite, hunger pangs at odd hours, diarrhoea or constipation, increased risk of indigestion and heartburn caused by eating meals at unusual hours when you would normally be asleep, and flare-ups of stomach ulcers.

Patients at risk of ulcers may find that alteration of circadian rhythm induces ulcers or makes them worse. The rhythm of stomach-acid production is different from the rhythm of natural mucus production protecting the stomach wall. Consequently, when these cycles readjust at different times, the stomach wall can be unprotected from the acid.

Your digestive system (appetite, acid secretion, enzyme secretion and bowel movements) may take up to twelve days to be resynchronized—or roughly one day for every time zone you cross.

Urinary system

This may be out of phase for up to ten days. Output of urine is usually less at night, but after travel you may be bothered by night-time visits to the toilet until you readjust.

Irritability and Depression

Many travellers feel irritable, and are affected by mood swings. These changes may be caused by disorientation and confusion, by insufficient sleep, daytime fatigue, or annoyance at feeling out of touch with surroundings or not in control. Almost a third of travellers report some degree of depression.

Headaches

These can be due to stress, or to a poorly-pressurized aircraft cabin causing a low concentration of oxygen in the blood, or to your body's response to turning night into day.

Alteration in Menstrual Cycles

Women who travel frequently, such as flight attendants, say that jet lag alters their menstrual cycles. Changes in time zones (and climate) can shorten, lengthen or even stop normal cycles, can increase or decrease menstrual flow and hinder ovulation. Periods can arrive early or late, or disappear for a month or more.

Tendency to catch colds

Some jet-setters complain of a greater susceptibility to catching colds and flu. Whether or not jet lag causes a depression of the body's immune system is still being debated and requires more research. This tendency may be attributable to the dry atmosphere of aircraft, which can dehydrate mucus membranes in nasal passages and make passengers more susceptible to infection. Or it may be due to a weakened condition due to stress and fatigue, high altitude, crowded airport terminals and the confined quarters of aircraft where viruses recirculate in air-conditioning systems.

Changes in the effectiveness of medicines

Some researchers have noted that disruptions of biological clocks caused by jet lag can aggravate some medical conditions or interfere with the effectiveness of certain medications. For instance, your heart rate may take five or six days to adjust, and if you take medicines, you may find they affect you differently—either less effectively or more strongly. This point is particularly important if you take any drugs on a strict daily dosage, such as those for hypertension, heart conditions or birth control.

Ageing

The effect of jet lag on the ageing process has not been studied in detail, but the case of a Pan American pilot has been noted: he accepted a five-year contract with British Overseas Airways on the route between London, Paris and Rome, after which he returned to Pan Am. He was shocked at the appearance of former colleagues: pilots who appeared typical for their age had been flying north-south routes whilst those who seemed to have aged considerably had spent the time on the more demanding west-east flights (see **Time zone factors**, below). Experimenters with mice, rats and hamsters concluded that constantly changing time zones reduced the animals' life-span.

How vulnerable will you be, and how quickly can you adjust?

Scientists have discovered that not only does your body have its own personal adjustment rate, but that each individual clock within your body has a different rate of adjustment. Although it takes only a moment to set your watch backward or forward to new time, it can take days or even weeks for your body clocks to reset if you haven't used the countermeasures in this guide.

Researchers say that most of us fall into three groups: *inert, intermediate* and *labile*. Inert people (about 15 per cent) are those whose body clocks are rigidly fixed, are least able to shift and take the most time to readjust. Labile people (another 15 per cent) are those who have inherited body clocks which are flexible and easily reset either backward or forward; they have the least trouble readjusting. Most of us fall into the intermediate category.

Your adjustment rate will be dependent upon the following factors.

Time zone factors

How many zones are you crossing?

Jet lag is only really noticeable if you have to cross three or more time zones. The greater the number of zones, the greater the jet lag and upheaval to your biological clocks. For instance, if you fly halfway around the world from London to Auckland, your jet-lag symptoms will last much longer and be more severe than if you go a shorter distance, crossing fewer meridians.

Conversely, if you had to fly nonstop around the world across twenty-four time zones, ending up precisely where you began, you would be extremely exhausted but your biological clocks would be unaffected.

Are you outward- or homeward-bound?
New studies indicate that if there are any differences in adjustment after outward or homeward flights, they are superficial and not really significant. Whether coming or going across several time zones, you will still suffer from jet lag to some degree.

Researchers used to believe that travellers were more affected by jet lag after flights taking them away from home rather than after trips coming back to home. They theorized that the well-established routines of home life helped travellers to resynchronize their body rhythms more quickly.

On the other hand, other travellers returning home from exciting holidays to boring jobs in a dreary environment, report a prolonged adjustment time.

Are you flying north, south, east or west?
If you fly in a *north-south* or *south-north* direction without any time-zone changes or alterations to your wrist-watch, you do not suffer jet lag.

Flying north   No time change   Flying south

You may be physically and mentally exhausted after a long flight in this direction but not jet-lagged. Some flights may be lengthy but do not cross to another time zone. For example, you can fly over three thousand miles from London to Accra, Ghana (see Appendix 1), taking seven hours but without altering your wrist-watch which remains on GMT. Or you can fly from New York to Panama (see Appendix 2), and remain on EST; 4.00 p.m. in New York is 4.00 p.m. in Panama; 10.00 a.m. in Sydney is 10.00 a.m in Port Moresby (see Appendix 3). You will disturb your sense of place, but your sense of time is unaffected, and you should adjust quickly. As soon as you have a good rest, you should overcome this simple travel fatigue.

East-west or *west-east* flights are not so simple. And the effects of east-west travel are different from west-east.

When you are *eastbound*, against the direction of the sun, you have to advance your wrist-watch and the flight day is shorter by that amount. Flying east causes more severe jet lag than flying west. In fact, you can take up to 50 per cent longer to recover from jet lag after an eastward flight than a westward flight of the same distance. Flying east, reducing the length of your flight day, is much more disruptive of subsequent natural cycles.

Flying east   Contracted flight day

When travelling *westward*, you are going in the same direction as the sun, you have to set your wrist-watch back and the flight day is longer by that amount. Flying west is not usually as disturbing to subsequent natural cycles as going east. Your body has a natural inclination to follow a sleep/wake cycle of about twenty-five hours, so this tendency to prolong the day fits well with a westward flight.

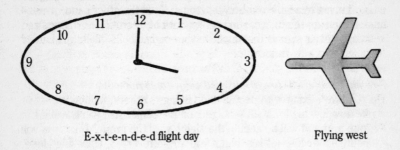

E-x-t-e-n-d-e-d flight day   Flying west

Personal factors

Your age

The younger you are, the less jet lag will bother you. Babies under three seem unaffected. Children can adjust more rapidly than their parents, and parents can adjust more rapidly than older people.

People over sixty can be troubled for weeks. The very elderly may already have fitful, disturbed or light sleep patterns that are very different from when they were middle aged, particularly if they have become more sedentary. Their body systems work less efficiently, with diminishing hormones and natural changes in body rhythms. On the other hand, when the elderly have their usual sleep/wake patterns disrupted by jet travel, the forced re-establishment of new body rhythms in a new time zone can often encourage better quality sleep throughout the night.

Your personality

You may have great determination and willpower, so although jet lag may be present, you can 'dismiss' it and force yourself to function to the best of your ability. Margaret Thatcher is a typical example of a person who simply does not give in to jet-lag symptoms; she claims she 'does not in general suffer from jet lag'. When you absolutely must attend an important international conference, or give a concert performance in a distant part of the world, or have booked the 'holiday of a lifetime', the importance of the situation can help you overcome jet-lag disturbances at least temporarily, far better than if you just yielded to jet lag without a fight.

Are you serene or anxious?
If you remain calm and composed in most difficult situations, it may be easier for you to adapt your body rhythms. If, on the other hand, you are anxious and apprehensive, your system may be secreting hormones and sending internal signals that unsettle your body clocks, making it harder to adjust to a new time zone.

Are you extroverted, gregarious and enjoy companionship?
Do you love mixing with people and talking to others, finding it easy to strike up conversation with strangers on the plane? Are you travelling in a group tour and will be seeing the sights with the group? If so, you will probably suffer less jet lag than if you are introverted, travelling alone, talking to no one throughout the flight, preferring to be alone in your room when you arrive, eating dinner by yourself and going sightseeing on your own.

Your habits
Do you like outdoor or indoor pursuits?
Jet lag's effects may be lessened if you are a regular walker or jogger. Researchers find that if you exercise outdoors as soon as you arrive, your inner body clocks will adjust more quickly and you are also less likely to suffer anxiety and depression.

Are you a 'short sleeper' or a 'long sleeper'?
Do you usually sleep seven hours or less each night—or nine hours or more? The fewer hours you generally sleep, the faster you should be able to adjust.

Are you flexible or regimented?
If you are very regular in your habits, used to living very precisely by the clock (rising, eating, going to bed at exactly the same hours each day), you may suffer less jet lag than if you are more flexible (getting out of bed at various hours, eating only when you feel like it, and going to sleep at any time).

Are you a 'lark' or an 'owl'?
An early riser, a morning lark, seems to adjust better when flying east; a night owl copes better when flying west. Which type are you? Are you an early riser and do your best work immediately you wake up? Or do you depend on an alarm clock, reach your peak performance about four

or five hours after waking, and prefer staying up late in the ordinary way?

Do you eat lightly or overeat?
Overeating can make jet lag worse. Heavy, rich meals may often be associated with business trips or luxury holidays, but eating too much and eating the wrong kinds of food at the wrong time of day or night can aggravate jet lag by burdening the liver and other digestive organs when they are out of phase.

Do you drink alcohol, smoke, or abstain?
Both smoking and drinking alcohol interfere with and slow down your inner clocks, prolonging readaptation to the time at your destination. When the aircraft is cruising at 35 000 feet, the cabin is pressurized to about 6 000 feet; altitude causes alcohol to reach your blood faster and it raises the blood alcohol level. Two drinks on the plane are at least as potent as three on the ground. They may be cheap—even free—but they increase chances of adding a hangover to your jet-lag trouble. Smoking and drinking interfere with your body's ability to process oxygen. Both add stress to your body during flight and can make a considerable difference in how you feel when you land. Alcohol and the cabin's heat and low humidity tend to dehydrate your body; dehydration makes it more difficult for body rhythms to adjust. Mixing alcohol and drugs while flying increases the power of both.

Your state of health
How much do you weigh?
Overweight people tend to be less bothered about disruption of normal mealtimes and less likely to suffer attacks of hunger pangs at unusual hours than thin people. The difference is small, however, and not a reason for putting on weight!

Are you in good health?
If you are normally in a delicate state of health, you may already have a disturbed biological rhythm. Poor health, exhaustion, sickness and chronic illnesses have their own impact on body clocks, so jet lag can put your body into an even more stressful condition that is slow to resynchronize. The disruption of body clocks can encourage or trigger mental illnesses and depression.

Do you regularly take medicines?
If you must take drugs for certain medical conditions, whether prescription or non-prescription, the timing of your dosages can be critical during flight or when you land, depending on when the drugs have to be taken if they are to be at their most effective. Medicines can lose some of their effectiveness, or even be detrimental, if taken at the wrong time of day or night. If you are stretching or contracting your 24-hour day by flying west or east, your doctor may advise adjusting dosage.

CHAPTER 2

BIOLOGICAL CLOCKS

What are biological clocks?

Jet lag's roots lie in the cyclical nature of the universe, cycles that are all around us, and have been since time began: day follows night, the moon waxes and wanes, the tides rise and fall, the seasons change. Internal rhythms are characteristic of all forms of life on Earth—rhythms that govern all aspects of behaviour, whether life is a single-cell organism or one of the larger mammals.

During the past thirty years, we have learned more about our inner clocks than during the rest of our time on Earth—information that is finally helping us to know what makes us tick and to beat jet lag. The study of this new area of biology, known as chronobiology, has accelerated now that jet travel is widespread.

For centuries, humans have observed and wondered at the rhythms around them and within their own bodies—natural rhythms in the environment that seemed to be linked to the rotation of the Earth, the orbit of the moon around the Earth, or the orbit of the Earth around the sun. Now scientists are demystifying these rhythms and reaching an understanding of the delicate and precise mechanisms by which sleep, physical function and reproduction in every living creature respond to the cycles of the solar day, the lunar month, the ocean tides, the terrestrial year—mechanisms as intricate as the clock on the wall or more complex human inventions.

Natural rhythms control the sprouting of seeds, tell birds when to sing, nest, mate, moult and migrate, and signal to animals the time to hibernate. They help birds, fish, crustaceans and insects to navigate; they help bees go from hives to flower pollen.

The light dawned when scientists realized that internal clocks compensate for the change in sunlight, increasing or decreasing several minutes each day with the changing seasons. Many of nature's cycles are seasonal or annual, and at the heart of them is *photoperiodism*. This is the way in which creatures sense the duration of daylight and position in the solar year, and stay in harmony with the environment, governing sense of time, sense of place and sense of well-being, in addition to the senses of sight, hearing, feeling, taste and smell. Clocks are part of genetic make-up, making the difference between survival and extinction in the natural world. Many people who work outdoors or enjoy outdoor sports can instinctively 'tell the time' by the angle of the sun and the surrounding shadows.

Originally, many human cycles were a means to survival, to keep us in sync with our environment, all regulated by inner mechanisms, all interrelated, and all disturbed by cross-meridian jet travel to a greater or lesser extent. The cycles can be of any length; for example:

Ultradian
More than once a day, such as heartbeat, pulse rate, breathing, cell division and brain waves.

Circadian
About a day, such as the sleep/wake pattern, temperature, hormone levels, blood-pressure, blood clotting, eyesight, mental ability, physical ability, sense of pain, digestion, bowel movements, urinary output, and metabolism.

Circaseptan
About once a week, such as blood-pressure, heartbeat, temperature and beard growth.

Circatrigintan or lunar
About once a month, such as hormone levels, ovulation and menstruation.

Circannual
About once a year, such as hormone levels and cell replacement.

Circadian or daily rhythms are the best known because they have been studied more extensively than the others, and appear to be the most disrupted by jet travel. They correspond to a solar day, regulating and organizing many occurrences in the body, and are naturally synchronized to the daily light/dark cycle.

The body's processes and functions occur in tide-like ebbs and flows (with male and female rhythms being roughly alike for the daily pattern), so that chemically you are a different person at noon from the one you are at night. Rhythms are evident in fluctuations of body temperature,

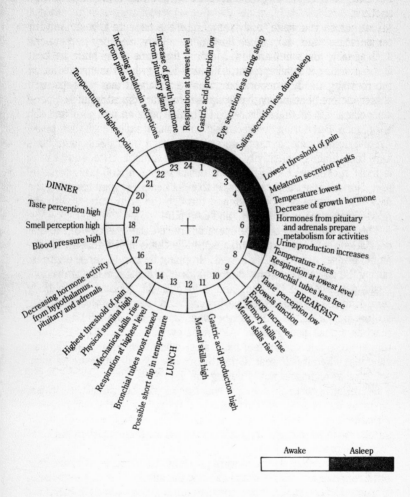

Figure 1: Principal activities of the average 24-hour biological clock

blood-pressure and heart activity, digestion, metabolism and cell division, mental sharpness, energy level and physical strength, within a cycle of eight hours' sleep and sixteen hours' wakefulness. The twenty-four hour clock in Figure 1 indicates some of the internal processes that fluctuate or oscillate in this daily pattern, and that are geared to one another.

Just before you wake, body temperature is near its lowest. As your temperature rises, hormones flow more quickly. Sensory perceptions such as taste and smell are low. Memory functions in the brain are best in the morning, declining towards midday. Energy levels increase during the morning. Body temperature rises to a plateau that it keeps until shortly before bedtime, with perhaps a temporary dip after lunch. Speed and accuracy in mental skills reach their high point around noon and ebb after lunch. But during the afternoon, mechanical skills reach their peak. Around dinner time, sensory perceptions are at their peak: taste buds have their highest sensitivity, sense of smell is most acute, and hearing is most receptive. Blood-pressure peaks between 5.00 p.m. and 7.00 p.m. Normal heartbeat can vary up to eight beats per minute during the day. The volume of blood pumped through the body varies, with the maximum between 10.00 a.m. and 6.00 p.m.

The rise and fall of body temperature once a day was one of the first oscillations to be studied in humans. Studies have shown that during the night, temperature is at its lowest, dropping by two to three degrees; during the day, temperature climbs and is at its highest in late afternoon, peaking between 2.00 p.m. and 4.00 p.m. In general, when body temperature becomes lower, performance and alertness also decrease, so that performance is lowest between 3.00 a.m. and 5.00 a.m., and reaches a peak near midday. Alertness cycles closely follow the body temperature curve. You feel most alert when temperature is highest; sleepiest when it is lowest. Growth hormone has the opposite pattern, secreted at night and rarely during the day.

Secretion of cortisol hormone, which helps your body deal with stress, normally peaks in early morning, close to waking, and declines in the evening near bedtime. Urine metabolism and potassium excretion peaks around midday, and is lowest during the night. Inner clocks control all these fluctuations.

Originally, biological clocks were probably only stimulated by the sun, so that circadian rhythms remain among the strongest cycles embedded in your body. Gradually, they evolved to run courses that broke away from the sun's influence. In studies of normal humans isolated in remote underground caves, cellars, and in special cubicles completely separated from external cues, scientists find that people's bodies establish their own natural cycles when left to their own devices, and are then called 'free-running'. These cycles are not twenty-four hours, in time with the sun. A few people have cycles as short as twenty-one hours; generally they are slightly longer, about twenty-five hours, so that many people tend naturally to sleep and wake up a little later each day if they don't have alarm clocks ringing loudly beside their beds. Studies of 'free-running' cycles have shown that women seem to have slightly shorter daily rhythms than men, and people who live on their own tend to have shorter rhythms than those who live with others, although researchers do not yet know why.

What keeps biological clocks on time?

If your daily cycle has a 'free-running' time of twenty-five hours rather than twenty-four, how do you synchronize to solar time? Your body can reset its clocks every day by means of *zeitgebers* (German: time-givers). *Zeitgebers* are cues that can be inside and outside your body, and also associated with your daily habits. For circadian rhythms, the most powerful stimulus is about sixteen hours of light and eight hours of darkness. Time-givers that help synchronize and reinforce the light stimulus are food, drinks, medicines, working, exercising, talking with others, and other social cues in a consistent daily pattern. Some cues you hear; some you see. Birds can act as cues when you're outdoors, with their daytime singing and night-time silence.

Living in a modern world, the regular time cues of our society and daily habits may be almost as important as those of nature: the shrill buzz of the alarm clock, the Greenwich time-signal on the radio, the booming tones of Big Ben. Church bells ringing for Mass or the muezzin calls for Muslim prayers. Traffic noise during the day; quiet streets at night. A nine-to-five job is a time cue, with the office-clock hands pointing to the lunch hour; later, the mantel clock indicates 11.00 p.m. or whenever it's time for bed.

Nerve pathways

The primary channel carrying external light/dark information leads from the retina layer at the back of the eyeballs along what scientists call the *retinohypothalamic tract* to a segment of the hypothalamus in the brain called the *suprachiasmatic nuclei* (SCN). These nerve connections between the eyes and the nuclei are independent of the pathways used for vision. The SCN are probably the principal mechanism for controlling circadian cycles, and are responsible for alertness during the day and sleepiness at night. They are formed and running in the human foetus as early as the seventh month of pregnancy, and set the lifetime rhythm for kidneys, heart, lungs and other organs.

Some of the body's rhythms don't depend entirely on the SCN. The adrenal glands, for example, appear to have a separate clock responsible for the secretion of the hormone cortisol.

The SCN consist of a pair of small egg-shaped clusters of 10 000 nerve cells, no more than a third of a millimetre in size—about the size of a pinhead—located in the front region of the hypothalamus. This master clock in the brain, linked to interrelated satellite time-keepers throughout the body, is cued by a certain minimum level of illumination and a certain spectrum of light. The brightness of light needed for the circadian system is much greater than the level you need to see by. And yellow light won't do; you need the total spectrum of 'white' light—the brilliance of sunlight or bright indoor lighting.

The pineal body

The SCN processes light signals from the eyes and fires off its own neural signals to organs such as the pineal. The pineal organ is not a gland, as many call it, but a converter of the SCN nerve signals into a hormonal output.

The pineal body, or *epiphysis cerebri*, is found in most vertebrates. The human pineal, situated deep between the brain's two hemispheres, is approximately 8 to 12mm long (0.31 to 0.47 inches), 4 to 8mm wide (0.15 to 0.31 inches), and is in the rough shape of a tiny pine cone. Most scientists had thought it was a vestigial part of our anatomy—a sort of 'appendix of the brain'. Some mystics called it a third eye and suggested it was part of the 'pathway to enlightenment', which was partly right.

Under conditions of darkness or low levels of light, the pineal is stimulated to secrete into the bloodstream the hormone *melatonin,* an indole compound—a chemical involved in sleep and fatigue (and one that also determines skin colour, hair colour and sexual development). Melatonin is produced in the pineal from a substance called serotonin, and serotonin is derived from L-tryptophan, an essential amino acid found in foods.

When light is sufficiently bright, the pineal responds by suppressing its production of melatonin, so the pineal tends to secrete small amounts of melatonin during the day and large amounts at night. The number of hours of daylight and darkness affect the amount of melatonin secreted, and therefore the daily wake/sleep cycle. Melatonin reaches its seasonal peak in the body during the long dark nights of winter. This is your own P.A. system—one of pineal activation.

The body-temperature pacemaker

One built-in time-keeper that takes its cue from the daily rhythm of your body temperature determines how long you sleep and regulates your arousal from sleep. This pacemaker notes when your temperature is at its lowest, in the early morning hours, and starts the mechanism to warm up your body, triggering your arousal from sleep until you wake.

If you're an early riser, or morning 'lark', your body temperature is probably lowest at around 3.00 or 4.00 a.m., two to three hours before you wake. If you're a night 'owl', you're likely to have your lowest body temperature at around 7.00 or 8.00 a.m. Most of us are somewhere in between. (In Mediterranean countries and other areas where the daily siesta is a habit, people's temperature rises and falls twice daily: they have a principal low at night and a secondary low around 3.00 or 4.00 p.m.)

What's the point of a built-in pacemaker? It gives you the same sort of jump on the day that you get with an automatic tea-maker. With this gadget you don't have to fumble in the morning to make tea; it's brewed and ready to go when you get up. In the same way, you don't waste the first part of the day preparing your own chemicals to rev up your brain and body. The predawn neuron and hormone signals of the biological clock act as 'on' and 'off' switches to start the chemical processes, taking two to three hours to warm the body to daytime levels, getting you perky for the day ahead, rather than waiting only for the external cues of dawn and dusk.

Natural chemicals for daytime activity

Your state of wakefulness during the daytime results from a combination of natural chemicals in the brain that send signals to keep you alert. A combination of the amino acid tyrosine, dihydroxyphenylalanine (L-DOPA), dopamine, norepinephrine and epinephrine, are produced by the body and trigger the adrenaline in your brain cells and other body systems to prepare you for the day's activities.

Natural chemicals for sleep

Your state of sleepiness depends on the adrenaline activity waning, and being replaced by the indole-amine signals to the brain from other chemical combinations that include L-tryptophan and serotonin. The indole-amine signals are the start of drowsiness and help you sleep.

To confuse all these mechanisms, all you have to do is step off an aircraft at some distant destination east or west after crossing several time zones. Being thrust into a different light/dark cycle and a changed environment confounds and upsets all the hundreds of internal clocks by giving altered external cues and creating considerable chemical disturbance of natural body chemicals.

If you have crossed several zones, inner confusion reigns. It may be daylight when you land, but your clocks may be shutting down your system expecting you to be asleep in bed. Or it may be total darkness at midnight at your destination, and your clocks are rousing you to be up, active and alert.

But harmony can be restored. When you know the secrets of chronobiology that allowed us to discover biological rhythms in the first place, you can beat jet lag!

CHAPTER 3

STRATEGY

There have been more theories on how to prevent and cope with jet lag than there are slides of your Uncle George's last holiday. Some of the theories are wild, most of them are unproven, and no one has yet invented a magic pill to take and *presto!*—jet lag's gone. But the Beat Jet Lag guidelines will help you with reliable, effective solutions, based on the latest scientific data.

Since we are all individuals with personally-timed circadian rhythms, different strategies and techniques can be used for various flight situations, varying personal needs, habits, motivation, lifestyle, health conditions, and reasons for travelling.

Where to start

You can beat jet lag at three basic stages of your journey: before flight, on flight day, and after flight. First use strategy: think before making a move.

Expect success

Don't self-sabotage. We all do it at times; some make a habit of it. Don't assume that you can't beat jet lag. You can. Definitely. But if you expect the worst, you hold yourself back, and fail even before you start. If you assume on your first day that you won't feel good, that you are going to be groggy during the day and won't sleep at night, you guarantee failure. Basically, you get what you expect. To overcome jet-lag blues, get the most out of a holiday or make a success of a business venture—expect to succeed: change your expectations by tapping the power of your imagination. With a positive attitude, you have determination, and give yourself a better chance of succeeding.

And don't sabotage yourself by leaving home feeling overtired. Before the flight, aim to start out well-rested: avoid late-night work or parties, hectic shopping or extra household chores.

Factors you cannot change

These factors include your age, your weight, your personality type (whether you like to socialize or prefer to be alone), the ingrained flexibility or adaptability of your circadian rhythms; whether you are a 'short sleeper' or a 'long sleeper', a 'lark' or an 'owl'; whether you suffer chronic diseases or disabilities.

Factors you can change
These factors include overeating and the types of foods and drinks you prefer, whether you drink or smoke, how much you exercise, and the positive efforts you make to be outdoors rather than indoors and to get a good night's rest.

Factor you may or may not change
This is the time-zone factor. You may have no choice about your planned destination. On the other hand, the route you take might be critical and could be changed to minimize jet lag, without unnecessary zigzagging across zones.

What your travel agent can do

Your travel agent or airline booking office can be your ally in the fight against jet lag. The right bookings can be crucial. Have a conference about where you want to go, how you want to travel, and how much time you have. You want to ask several questions:

● is a time-zone change necessary?
● are there alternative routes?
● what choice do you have for the time of the flight departure?
● what is the length of the flight?
● what choice do you have for the time of arrival?
● is there a tour group you can join?
● is there a less-crowded flight?
● what meals will be served during the flight?
● is a planned stopover a smart move?

Time zones
Ask your travel agent if a time change is necessary; if so, how many hours; and check whether Daylight Saving Time is in effect at your destination when calculating the time difference. Flying eastward, you will have to advance your watch. If you're heading west, you will set your watch back.

Routes

Try to travel westwards when possible, to reduce jet lag symptoms. If your trip is around the world, fly in a westerly direction.

Departures

Don't lose sleep over it. Ideally, you want to pick a flight that doesn't force you to rise earlier than usual, say before 5.00 or 5.30 in the morning, that would deprive you of sleep before you start. You also want to travel during the daytime, during the active phase of your body clocks.

For a short trip eastbound, choose a flight early in the day; for a longer flight eastbound, book a late plane that leaves before midnight and plan to sleep during the flight. For a short trip westbound, plan to depart later in the day; for a longer trip westbound, schedule an early departure.

Arrivals

Arrange to arrive at your destination in the late afternoon or early evening, so you are not compelled to stay up late, but just in time for a good night's sleep. If flights are limited only to very late arrivals, plan to fly a day earlier to give yourself R & R and sleep for a day prior to your appointments.

'Red-eye' flights

Don't be tempted to book a 'red-eye' special that transfers you overnight to your destination like a bag of airmail. It's true that you save the expense of a costly hotel room, and may reduce the length of your absence from the office, but a night arrival creates disastrous confusion of your inner mechanisms and prolongs their readjustment. If you reach your destination when it would be between midnight and 6.00 a.m. at your departure point, you are at the lowest point of your activity phase. Your biological clocks are still telling you to sleep at a time when you need to be active and alert for disembarking, claiming luggage, dealing with Immigration, Customs, foreign money exchange and hailing a taxi to your hotel. In addition, when you arrive early and need to check into a hotel, the chances are the room won't be ready for occupancy until after 11.00 a.m., and you are likely to spend time sitting in the hotel reception lobby.

Red-eye flights can be unpredictable: sometimes empty, sometimes full, in which case you gamble on being condemned to spend the night sleeping bolt-upright. These disadvantages and discomforts will intensify jet-lag symptoms at your destination. Unless your schedule makes a night flight imperative, or impossible to avoid, your best choice is a flight with a more sensible arrival time.

Standby fares

These may also be a tempting way to economize, by slicing ticket prices up to fifty per cent, but they are also a way to have last-minute rushes, insecurity and anxious moments that compound jet-lag problems.

Group tours

When making your booking, consider a group tour. Travelling in a crowd, you spend more time talking and socializing with the others, rather than being on your own. Studies have shown that people in group tours are particularly better at fighting jet lag than those who travel alone.

A less-crowded flight

Ask the travel agent or airline office if some flights on the route you want are less than full. Then when you board, you can often find two or three seats together to stretch out for sleep.

What meals will be served?

If the flight you choose is scheduled to serve breakfast, lunch or dinner, major airlines usually offer as many as eighteen alternative choices (such as vegetarian, Hindu, kosher, low-calorie and low-cholesterol). Ask the agent to book a meal selection that will tie in with the food recommendations in Chapter 5 (high protein or high carbohydrate) and the Beat Jet Lag Plans in Chapter 6.

Planned stopovers

For a trip that crosses many time zones, plan the journey to include several stopovers. Your travel agent can probably write the tickets so that you don't have to pay a surcharge for the privilege of spending a night or so in intermediate cities en route. Many major airports around the world have sleeping rooms for travellers, usually situated in the terminal building. Some airlines now make free overnight rooms a standard feature if you are a first-class or business-class passenger with a connecting flight the next day. Air France, for example, offers its passengers a room at a top Paris hotel for those continuing on within twenty-four hours to Africa, Europe or the Middle East. Finnair's first- and business-class travellers connecting through Helsinki can have a free night at a hotel, or if they have less time, they can choose to relax in a sauna for a few hours.

With more time and money, you can take an even more leisurely pace to cross several time zones or circle the globe. In this way, elderly travellers on holiday can enjoy long journeys that are relatively unstressful, even though they are at an age when jet lag can produce the greatest disruption of biological clocks. By breaking the journey into several flights of no more than two or three time zones per flight, the stopovers help the body readjust gradually to a new time frame and reduce the impact of jet lag. This was President Richard Nixon's approach when he embarked on his historic mission to China; the stops he made in Hawaii and Guam were to ensure that he would arrive at his destination well-prepared and adjusted—physically and mentally.

Cruising, Fly/Cruising and Fly/Drive
Crossing time zones by ship or by road gives you easy leisurely resynchronization. Nearly half the major cruise lines offer air/sea packages on some or all of their sailings. If you are going to book one of these flight/cruise or fly/drive packages, fly westwards, and cruise or drive eastwards, if possible. Use the Beat Jet Lag Plan for the westbound flight. If cruising or driving west and flying home east, you will need the Beat Jet Lag Plan for the eastbound flight.

'Milk-runs' or non-stops
A 'milk-run' flight with too many intervening stops can be tiring and tiresome, with prolonged fatigue in addition to jet lag.

Most travellers want a quick non-stop flight direct to their final destination. This is when careful strategy is needed. The precautions you take (or don't take) before departure can determine whether the holiday or business trip proves to be a success or failure. These methods can be described as 'political manoeuvres' to suit certain situations, since they are often used by leading politicians.

Political manoeuvres

Hometown time
When the whole trip is of short duration, or if you have multiple destinations within a short time period, plan to stay with your hometown time. You may want to cross the Atlantic by Concorde for a business luncheon in New York, and be back in your own bed the same night. Rather than trying to adapt your biological clocks for a day or two, it may be more effective to maintain London time: don't reset your watch, keep it set at GMT. (But if you do book the Concorde to New York and want to remain *several* days, use the Beat Jet Lag Plans in Chapter 6, as you

would with any subsonic jet.) Or if you live in Washington DC and need to spend only two or three days in Paris then fly home, don't worry about adjusting—you won't be away long enough to make the adjustment worthwhile.

It may take some determination to keep your body attuned to home time, as your activities could be out of phase with the local population, but no biological adjustment is necessary. Get plenty of sleep, then schedule your business meetings during your normal active daytime phase, at times that coincide with the active phase of the people you are visiting. High officials have been known to insist that talks be conducted on *their* time rather than that of the meeting place. President Lyndon Johnson adopted this technique—but then a man in his position could assume that others would fit in with him without question! Orbiting astronauts also use this system: spacecraft are kept in time with the Johnson Space Center in Houston for the duration of space missions, so that astronauts don't have to cope with the stress caused by dysrhythmia in addition to the biological changes due to weightlessness.

You may find it convenient to wear *two* watches: keep one on GMT (or whatever is 'hometown time'), which you follow for eating meals at your usual hours and for sleeping at your usual time; and set the other watch on trip time for appointments at your destination(s).

Doing the shift
This method was used by Dr Henry Kissinger during his 'shuttle diplomacy': a day or two immediately before departure, shift your sleep cycle to equal the time zones to be crossed, and help shift your biological clocks to your destination time-frame before boarding the jet. It's a good strategy to follow if you have five or more time zones to cross. Your clocks won't be fully adjusted, but you will make a start in the right direction. Before flying west from New York to Los Angeles, for example, stay up an hour or so later at night, sleep a little longer in the morning, and take your meals at times later than usual. Before the return journey coming east, go to bed an hour or so earlier, and set your meals at earlier times.

Time Allowance
Give yourself T-I-M-E. Plan to arrive several days before attending meetings and conferences, or competing in sports events to reduce jet-lag symptoms and become more adjusted. Don't be tempted to go straight to an important meeting to show everybody how tough you are. Government officials and business leaders are routinely advised to

recover from jet lag before starting conferences or sensitive negotiations.

Some years ago, President Dwight D. Eisenhower used this technique. More recently, Soviet President Mikhail Gorbachev used it for a tactical advantage when he met President George Bush at the Malta Summit Meeting in 1989: from Moscow he flew west to Rome (the same zone as Malta) three days before talks with Bush, who arrived just before the meeting after a six-zone eastward time-shift.

Athletes travelling across three or more time zones to compete in international events need to take extra precautions to be at the peak of fitness and give the best performance; other factors apart from jet lag can affect physical ability, such as differences in climate and altitude. Arrive several days early at the site of the event, especially if the sport involves muscle strength, endurance, and concentration, such as wrestling, running and football.

There are various ways to estimate a time allowance. As a general guide, allow twenty-four hours for each two hours of time difference. For example, after flying from Los Angeles to London (eight time zones), allow four full days to adjust.

Another way to calculate time allowance is to use Buley's Rest-Stop Formula. The formula, named after Dr L.E. Buley, former Chief of the Aviation Medicine Section of the International Civil Aviation Organization, is calculated like this:

$$\frac{\text{Rest period}}{\text{(in tenths of days)}} = \frac{\text{Travel time (hrs.)}}{\text{divided by 2}} + \frac{\text{Time zones}}{\text{in excess of 4}} + \frac{\text{Departure}}{\text{Coefficient}} + \frac{\text{Arrival}}{\text{Coefficient}}$$

This formula is simply that the rest period (expressed in tenths of days) equals the sum of one-half the flight duration, plus the number of time zones crossed in excess of four, plus two special coefficients representing departure and arrival times. The coefficients reflect the favourability or unfavourability of local times and are derived from the following table:

Departure		Arrival	
Local time	Coefficient	Local time	Coefficient
8.00-11.59 a.m.	0	8.00-11.59 a.m.	4
12.00-5.59 p.m.	1	12.00-5.59 p.m.	2
6.00-9.59 p.m.	3	6.00-9.59 p.m.	0
10.00 p.m.-0.59 a.m.	4	10.00 p.m.-0.59 a.m.	1
1.00-7.59 a.m.	3	1.00-7.59 a.m.	3

First, find out how long your flight will take (using the Appendices, the current Airline Guide or by asking your travel agent). If you are crossing four or fewer than four time zones, omit this figure from the formula.

So let's suppose that you are flying from Los Angeles to London: the eleven-hour flight across eight time zones leaves at 7.00 p.m. and arrives in London at 2.00 p.m. local time the next day.

$$\text{Rest period} = \frac{11}{2} + 4 + 3 + 2 = 14.5 \text{ or } 1.45 \text{ days.}$$

The rest period calculated from this formula should be rounded to the nearest higher half-day, so the above example prescribes that you should not work for one and a half days after arrival in London.

This system is used, in its original or a modified form, by a number of governmental and international organizations, including the U.S. State Department, the U.S. Federal Aviation Administration, Canadian Forces Air Transport Command, Alcan Aluminium Limited, Campbell Soup Company, I.B.M. Corporation, Continental Oil, Shell Oil and Phillips Petroleum. The medical officers of many large firms insist that their top executives schedule no crucial meetings or appointments on the day of their arrival after a flight with a time-zone difference of several hours, particularly on eastbound flights. No serious business should be conducted in the first twenty-four hours unless there has been a rest or sleep cycle. Many companies suggest that older employees take at least two days' rest after flight, to allow for adjustment; some firms advise personnel to arrive just before a weekend. Two or three days are usually insufficient for full adjustment to a new time zone if you have travelled across more than six, unless you take the other countermeasures to influence body clocks in the Beat Jet Lag Plans in Chapter 6.

If several business appointments have you zigzagging to numerous airports around the world and multiple destinations, be sure to space out meetings sufficiently far apart to give yourself a time allowance after arrival at each destination and before the start of each meeting—otherwise *you'll* be 'spaced out'. An alternative is to remain on your hometown time for multi-destination flights, as described earlier.

CHAPTER 4

LIGHTS! ACTION!

Light, and lots of it, is one of the key ingredients in setting human clocks. The sun is our essential and most powerful *zeitgeber.*

Around 4.5 thousand million years ago, the sun flared into life, to energize the Earth, to drive the weather and, in myriad ways, to govern the very existence of all terrestrial life. In ages past, people worshipped the sun as the bountiful provider; in the jet age, we now know it helps us to Beat Jet Lag.

There's more to sunshine than meets the eye. Sunshine not only gives pleasure by increasing your sense of well-being, warming your skin, and giving a tan. The sun's light reaches beyond your eyes and sends messages to your brain and body. Bright light alone can rapidly reset the human circadian rhythm in two to three days after it has been disturbed by long-distance multiple time-zone flights. The human biological clock is much more responsive to light than scientists had previously suspected. Since the mid-1970s, many researchers had held the view that humans were not sensitive to light resetting, and had not believed that body clocks could be fooled into thinking night is day and day is night. Many thought that people's circadian rhythms were synchronized mainly by social contact, but recent studies show that our internal clocks do indeed respond to light in a fundamental way.

What you can do

On flight day
Since sunlight is the strongest *zeitgeber* that your body can have, learn to use the on/off switch whenever you need light exposure and whenever you don't, to trick your body into thinking it is already in the new time zone.

If your flight occurs during what would be your *daytime/active* phase at your destination, control your light cues on the aircraft during your trip by using natural or artificial light. Keep window blinds open. Keep reading lights on.

Keep your *brain* active: talk to fellow passengers, listen to lively music on your personal stereo, watch the in-flight movie, play a mind-stimulating game of cards with a companion, do a challenging crossword puzzle—or work with your briefcase on the pull-down table in front of you.

Keep your *body* active: pace the aisles, do Energizing Exercises (see box), and get up frequently for drinking water.

If it would be *night time* at your destination but the sunshine is streaming through the cabin window, trick your body into believing that it is night time: pull down the blinds, shut off the overhead lights, ignore the airline meals, movies and stereo music. Minimize talking. Cover your eyes with an eye-mask, get under a blanket, and sleep or relax (see Chapter 7). If you can't sleep, wear dark glasses to prevent your eyes from seeing daylight from other cabin windows or other people's reading lights.

After flight

After a long flight, you will naturally be tired. Even if your fatigue is not directly due to jet lag, you will feel the strain of sitting cooped up in the aircraft cabin for hours.

If you arrive at night time, turn off room lights and shut your eyes until sunrise. Set your alarm clock for daybreak at the new time zone, or ask the hotel staff to wake you at dawn. If you are hard of hearing, get a flashing-light clock for an alarm, or a clock-radio which you set on high volume. Clock-radios don't wind down or stop; they blast away until you get up to face the day.

If you land during the daytime, though the temptation may seem irresistible to take a nap as soon as you reach your hotel room—*don't*! You'll only prolong jet lag. Freshen up with a quick shower, a brisk towelling, a shave or splash of cologne, then leave your room and *go outdoors*. When you feel tired, researchers recommend that you spend more time in bright light rather than sleeping. Drowsiness disappears as daytime neurotransmitters send their signals through your body. If eyelids start to droop or eyes begin to burn, get outside. Surround yourself with the new light, new sights and new sounds, and be in step with your destination. Be out in the light and see the brightness. Don't look directly *at* the sun, of course, or you will damage your eyes. Shade your eyes with a sun visor if you like, but *don't* wear sunglasses. You want the sunlight to reset your biological clock. Spend as much time as possible outdoors for the first couple of days at your destination, and use your 'personal P.A. system' (pineal activation). As the light rays reach your eyes, they will send the message through to your brain to suppress melatonin secretions. (For skin protection, wear a wide-brimmed hat,

Energizing Exercises

These are designed to be performed in a seated position during the flight and after the flight, during the active phase at your destination, whenever you want to stay active or need to renew your vitality.

1. Deep breathing, repeat six times: breathe deeply, to replace and refresh the air in your lungs and bring fresh oxygen to your blood. Oxygen is a potent clock adjuster.
2. Stretching, repeat six times: raise your arms above your head to 'pick apples'. *Stretch* up your body, *lift* your torso, and hold for one minute.
3. Neck movements and head nodding, repeat six times: slowly turn your head to the left, hold; look straight ahead, hold; turn to the right, hold; then straight again. Slowly let your head fall on your chest, to feel the stretch at the back of your neck; then hold your head back, chin up, to feel the stretch at your throat.
4. Shoulder movements, repeat six times: bring both shoulders forward, then back, describing large circles in both directions.
5. Wrist stimulation, repeat ten times: turn your hands all the way over and spread your fingers, then twist in the other direction.
6. Ankle stimulation, repeat ten times: rotate your feet in large circles, as far as they can turn.
7. Blood stimulation, repeat ten times: bring your left knee up towards your right elbow, then your right knee up towards your left elbow.
8. On the spot jogging, for two minutes: raise your arms in a bent position and swing them backwards and forwards as if walking vigorously.
9. Blood stimulation, repeat ten times: rise from your seat and then sit, without the help of your hands.
10. Blood stimulation, repeat ten times: pull in your stomach and bend forward; then relax stomach muscles and straighten up.

and use a sunscreen cream with a factor of SPF-15, available at the chemist. Pack your own to be sure of supplies. Serious sunburn is common if you are in the tropics.) As soon as your inner clocks have readjusted, you can resume wearing sunglasses outdoors, to protect your eyes from possible ultraviolet B radiation.

Time your light dose

Researchers at the Oregon Health Sciences University of Portland have devised a schedule of light exposure in mornings and afternoons, to reset inner clocks and function in a new environment. Similar strategy can help you adapt after your return flight.

After flying from west to east, be outdoors in bright light in the *morning* to advance your daily rhythms, to get a day's dose of light and be more prepared to accept an earlier bedtime. For instance:

West to East

Time difference from departure point:	Stay indoors: (local time)	Be outdoors: (local time)
2 hours	—	6.00 a.m.-8.00 a.m.
4 hours	—	6.00 a.m.-10.00 a.m.
6 hours	—	6.00 a.m.-12.00 noon
8 hours	6.00 a.m.-8.00 a.m.	8.00 a.m.-2.00 p.m.
10 hours	6.00 a.m.-10.00 a.m.	10.00 a.m.-4.00 p.m.
12 hours	12.00 noon-6.00 p.m.	6.00 a.m.-12.00 noon

If you have been flying from east to west, delay exposure to sunlight until later in the day, to shift your daily rhythms backward, in time with the new zone. Bright light exposure in the *afternoon* appears to delay bodily rhythms so that the need for sleep comes later. For instance:

East to West

Time difference from departure point:	Stay indoors: (local time)	Be outdoors: (local time)
2 hours	—	4.00 p.m.-6.00 p.m.
4 hours	—	2.00 p.m.-6.00 p.m.
6 hours	—	12.00 noon-6.00 p.m.
8 hours	4.00 p.m.-6.00 p.m.	10.00 a.m.-4.00 p.m.
10 hours	2.00 p.m.-6.00 p.m.	8.00 a.m.-2.00 p.m.
12 hours	12.00 noon-6.00 p.m.	6.00 a.m.-12.00 noon

Even if it is cloudy or raining, be sure you are outside during the specified hours as the timing is important. The above tables are devised for flights between cities where sunlight lasts twelve hours, sunrise is at 6.00 a.m. and sunset at 6.00 p.m. If daylight is not available between these hours, you should use bright indoor light as a substitute.

If you must remain indoors on your first day or two for meetings or conferences, keep all the room lights on, position yourself near the lamps, move your desk or worktable close to the window, and keep curtains or window-blinds fully open.

Activities that get you out in the bright sunshine or daylight provide the quickest way to fresh adjustment of circadian cycles. Where can you go? What can you do? If you have a report to complete before a meeting, finish it while sitting outside. Better still, take a stroll or short jog around the city, have a swim at the beach or outdoor pool, sip a cool drink at a sidewalk café, have a picnic or relax in the park. From a park bench, you can recover from jet lag and readjust from cultural shock, reinforcing your social cues and sound cues as you talk with local people, watch children playing, hear birds singing, church bells tolling the hours, or the traffic roaring by.

All cities have at least one park; many have scenic promenade walks along rivers or lakeside. Visitors to London can walk along the Thames Embankment, take cruises up and down the river, walk in Hyde Park, Regents Park, Kew Gardens and the Zoo. Paris has her *jardins*, the Bois de Boulogne, and walks along the River Seine; you can cruise Amsterdam's canals, walk through the Prater in Vienna and beside the Lake in Geneva; Moscow has Gorky Park. In Hong Kong, take the ferry across the harbour to soak up the Oriental scene from a hill overlooking the South China Sea. In Sydney, go to the wonderful Zoo and fabulous beaches; and in Auckland, tour the harbour, take in the view at One Tree Hill, or go to the Ellerslie Racecourse. After a flight to New York, take the excursion boat to the Statue of Liberty, or go to the top of the Empire State Building. In Washington, D.C., walk along the Potomac River, and in San Francisco, cruise around the Bay or walk in Golden Gate Park. Mexico City has Chapultepec Park, and Rio de Janeiro has its famous beaches and Sugarloaf Mountain. Wherever you are, there are things to do outside so that you absorb those light rays and socialize with other people.

Studies have shown that jogging may be as good for your circadian system as it is for the circulation. Large hotels in major cities around the world can provide jogging maps showing various local routes—ask the concierge or receptionist. When in Moscow, you can jog around the

Kremlin, and in Leningrad, along the quay facing the Gulf of Finland. If you find yourself in China, you can run for miles along the Great Wall, or join the locals in *T'ai Chi* outdoor exercises. When in Tokyo, try the jogging route that encircles the Imperial Palace—Japanese businessmen are running too, and will greet you in passing with a slight ceremonial bow at full speed.

In the open air, you are consciously and subconsciously taking it all in, with *zeitgebers* all around you. These activities are not only relaxing, but more importantly, they help to speed your readjustment of inner rhythms by as much as 50 per cent. Travel agents and group leaders can help in this regard by rearranging sightseeing itineraries and putting *outdoor* activities at the start of organized tours, wherever possible.

Whether or not you are travelling with a group, talk with as many people as possible during your new hours of wakefulness on the first day or two, to enter wholeheartedly into life at your destination and increase the cues you receive by socializing with others: ask directions, talk to shopkeepers, share a lunch table, or try out a newly-acquired language. These social cues reinforce the sunlight/darkness cues you receive and will speed readjustment. If you remain relatively isolated, you'll take longer to adjust to the new time frame.

What you *don't* want to do is remain inside, with room-service meals. Hidden away, alone in a hotel room, you don't even begin to adjust to cues from light, time and society. And you don't need darkened cinemas and theatres, or light-dimmed museums and churches during your first couple of days. Save them for later in the trip when you have better adjusted your internal clocks and no longer feel daytime drowsiness.

Pre-adjustment in the future

Researchers are now predicting that future passengers will be resetting their inner clocks by one or two hours per night, *before* departing on a long transmeridional flight, by using commercial light boxes. Light-therapy kiosks will become standard equipment for passengers at major airports. You will have a shot of light before takeoff, with your personal 'light therapy' card telling you the best time to have it.

Recent experiments show that exposure to a light stimulus at *night* will bring a greater response from your neuroendocrine system and dramatically reduce readjustment time.

If you have ever been awakened for an emergency at three o'clock in the morning, you know the feeling of being forced alert before you are ready: the phone rings, you fumble, and snapping on a light makes you shudder. We take pleasure in sunshine during the daytime in our active phase, but detest it at night during our inactive phase. New studies show that by exposing people to artificial bright light during the night, when body temperature is at its lowest, circadian clocks can be readjusted by several hours. Scientists are finding that people are four times as sensitive to light at night than during the day, so that to reset the biological clock forwards, the traveller will be exposed to light after the middle of the night, and to move it backwards, a traveller will receive light during the first half of the night.

What measure of light might you need? Some experiments have used 10 000 lux; others as little as 2 500 lux (see box). In a recent study, groups of people were given three days of treatments, with five hours of intense light, about 10 000 lux each day, at various times during their internal cycles.

How Light is Measured

What is a lux?

Illumination and the measurement of light is expressed in *lumens* in the United Kingdom, and in *foot-candles* in the United States of America. One lumen per square foot is the amount of light given by one candela (originally, a wax candle) at a distance of one foot (30 centimetres). In European countries and in the scientific community, the corresponding metric unit is the *lux*, that is, one lumen per square metre. One lumen per square foot is equivalent to 10.76 lux, or very approximately 10 lux. The full moon is equal to one-third of a lux. In your office, you probably have a few hundred lux. Overall fluorescent lighting used in factories is about 1 000 lux. The intensity of light at sunrise, or unobstructed daylight from a bright overcast sky, gives about 10 000 lux, and midday sunshine measures 100 000 lux.

The experiments reset internal clocks by as much as twelve hours, in a complete reversal of sleep-wake phases. The therapy involves not only the exposure to bright light but requires the correct *timing* of the exposure to get the right response. The rapid resetting of inner clocks works like this:

On the first day, a dose of strong light suppresses circadian variations to make them irregular. That is, changes in body temperature throughout the day are smaller than normal. The second day's dose drastically reduces them. And with the clocks in a sort of limbo, the third light dose on the following day restarts the pacemakers to new active/inactive time phases.

Sometime in the future, your travel agent may give you a special 'light therapy' card showing what is known as a 'phase response curve': a drawing that indicates how much your clock might be reset, depending on when you have light exposure, from which you could see the best time to use light to reset your clock. The card might look similar to the one shown in Figure 2:

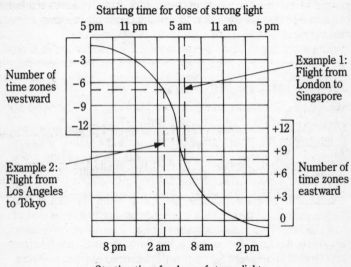

Figure 2: Experimental Light Therapy

In Example 1, if you plan to fly from London to Singapore, eight hours ahead, the light therapy card might indicate that your light exposure should be around 6.30 a.m. London time. (Where the plus 8-hour line intersects the curve, you read up to find the time.)

Or, in Example 2, if you fly from Los Angeles to Tokyo, and need to set your clock back seven hours, the graph might show that you should be exposed to strong light at about 3.00 a.m. Los Angeles time. (Where the minus 7-hour line intersects the curve, you read down to find the time.)

Much more clinical study and investigation needs to be done to determine correct dosage and timing of artificial light. The experimental studies completed so far have been done with young men; the results may be different for women and for other age groups, and short flights may be different to long ones.

Going to a tanning booth won't do you any good because that light is ultraviolet. For biological clock resetting you need white or full-spectrum lights, similar to sunlight. Full-spectrum lights artificially create sunlight, and send the right signals to your body to suppress melatonin production when you need jet-lag adjustment or feel gloomy and depressed in the middle of winter. The way of the future will be light-therapy kiosks equipped with specialized lamps and staffed by professional light-therapists, and perhaps aircraft with new seating sections equipped with banks of bright lights—'Light Class'—to reset the jet set.

Playing around with bright lamps is *not* a Do-It-Yourself job, though, as you can severely damage your eyes and vision if intense light is carelessly used. For more information on light therapy, readers are recommended to write to:

Society for Light Treatment and Biological Rhythms, Inc., 722 West 168th Street, Box 50, New York, NY 10032.

Or to: **Lighting Research Institute**, 345 East 47th Street, New York, NY 10017.

In the meantime, sunshine is free. If you spend the first two days outdoors after a long flight, six to eight hours of bright sunlight should do the trick, along with the other countermeasures in the Beat Jet Lag Plans.

CHAPTER 5

LET'S EAT!
LET'S DRINK!

Other tools to reset your inner mechanisms and effectively beat jet lag are foods and drinks. Foods can be friends or foes, drinks can be allies or enemies.

Foods

One of the major points in the Beat Jet Lag Plans is having the right food at the right time—not a fad diet, not giving up favourite foods, but knowing the best time of day to eat them. For fast results, you want real food to energize your body, stimulate your mind, during your active daytime phase. The right food improves your ability to overcome jet lag, and is absolutely vital when embarking on extensive travel when you need to be extra alert, active, and adjusted rapidly to new time phases.

Scientists can now measure every compound in food in minute quantities, track the flow of these natural chemicals throughout the body, and analyse their effect right down to basic molecules and their mechanisms. Recent scientific breakthroughs have shown that when food chemicals reach the brain—interacting with neurotransmitters—they have a direct and far-reaching effect on the state of your health, your mind, and the amount of energy that reaches your muscles.

Knowing this, you can signal a more rapid resynchronization of inner clocks by deliberately eating certain foods known to give positive results. You can rev up your energy and give a boost to your mental alertness and mood by carefully choosing foods that can act as natural stimulants to mental alertness, memory and energy, *or* foods that work as simple tranquillizers or antidepressants, to calm anxieties and make you drowsy—just when you want to be, to switch your biological clocks over to the new local time.

One way scientists track the effect of different foods is by monitoring blood glucose levels. Your blood contains about 85mg of glucose per 100ml of blood when you wake in the morning. This is called the fasting glucose level and is normal. Then when you eat a meal containing protein, carbohydrates or fats, the glucose level responds to these different nutrients. (See the graph in Figure 3.)

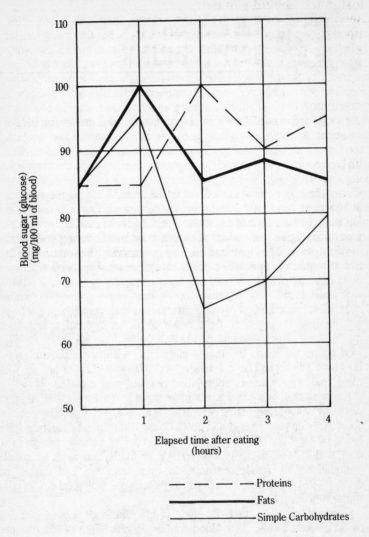

Figure 3: Blood Sugar Levels

The crucial factors in beating jet lag with foods are *what* foods you eat, *how much* you eat and *when* you eat them.

How much should you eat?

Overeating can make jet lag worse. Heavy, rich meals are often associated with business trips and luxury holidays, but they aggravate jet lag by burdening the liver and other organs in the digestive tract just when these organs are out of phase. You need to eat lightly, on the day before you travel, on flight day, and a day or two after flight, so that your digestive clock is gently ticking over—never burdened—while it is out of phase and readjusting.

Although some swear by diets of high/low calories on alternate days to combat jet lag, many scientists remain sceptical. The original experiments used laboratory animals, but there are no controlled studies with humans to prove that such programmes work. Having gone through complicated procedures of a travel diet, people may talk themselves into believing that the regimen made them feel better—the placebo effect. But huge amounts of food and thousands of calories are too much for people of slight build, slow metabolism, small appetite and little physical activity. Large meals overload the digestive system and play havoc with a weight-loss diet. It's better to have a minimum of food in small portions—portions that your digestive tract finds easier to cope with.

When should you eat?

Ideally, you want to start your Beat Jet Lag Plan before you leave, and match meal times with those at your destination. Failing that, begin the programme during the flight. The snag is that plane meal times don't always coincide with your destination meal times; airlines serve meals to fit flight schedules and the convenience of their busy flight attendants. It's true that on certain airlines and certain routes, food service is more flexible now, so that passengers can choose what they want to eat and when to eat it. But if the flight attendant serves a large dinner at two in the morning when you are trying to sleep, ask him or her to bring the tray later, more in time with your personal destination.

Whether you are in the air or have already landed, the Beat Jet Lag Plan recommends that you eat your biggest meal at breakfast, a smaller amount at lunch, and your smallest at dinner. Years ago, your mother may have said "Eat your breakfast. It's the most important meal of the day". It still makes sense when you want to beat jet lag successfully.

What should you eat?

The Beat Jet Lag Plan fights the jet-setter's two main problems: daytime drowsiness and night-time insomnia. When you are following the Plan, you don't have to deny yourself any particular food—just be sure that you eat it at the right time of day.

Early in the day you need *proteins* in foods to tell your brain and other organs in your body to rev up and stimulate the production of natural chemicals—to re-establish the adrenaline channels that start your day, for physical energy and mental alertness, giving them a boost at the beginning of the *new* active phase in your new twenty-four-hour cycle. Avoid fatty foods when you must be mentally alert. Then towards evening, you need *carbohydrates* in foods to send other messages along the indole-amine channels to your brain, telling you to slow down, become drowsy and sleepy—ready for the *new* inactive phase.

If you are under doctor's orders about your diet, ask the physician's opinion on the high-protein breakfasts and lunches followed by high-carbohydrate suppers. If certain foods are taboo, perhaps your doctor or dietitian will advise a slightly-modified Plan for you.

For stimulating the adrenaline channels, a meal high in proteins (see box) will give you energy and food for thought for up to five hours.

Proteins to energize mind and muscle

Best choices, high in protein and low in fat, are:

- Lean roast or boiled beef, with no visible fat.
- Lean ham or gammon.
- Grilled chicken or turkey (with skin removed).
- Grilled fish, boiled shellfish (with no high-fat batter coatings).
- Boiled or poached eggs.
- Low-fat cottage cheese.
- Low-fat yogurt.
- Skimmed or low-fat milk.
- Tofu (soya bean curd).

How do proteins work for you? They increase alertness and help you feel more energetic because they introduce the amino acid *tyrosine* into your body (fish and shellfish being particularly good sources). Tyrosine, in turn, stimulates the production of the brain's alertness chemicals, *dopamine* and *norepinephrine*. But if a high-protein food is also high in fat, it won't boost your mental energies, and the fat slows the absorption of protein into your body. Fatty foods take longer to digest than other foods, and cause more blood to drain from the brain to your stomach—and *that* process slows down your thinking and makes you sluggish.

For triggering the indole-amine channels to prepare you for sleep, eat foods high in carbohydrates (see box), to put you in a more relaxed frame of mind. A meal high in carbohydrates and low in protein and fat increases insulin in the blood and triggers a greater ratio of the chemical *tryptophan*. Tryptophan in the brain activates the neurotransmitter *serotonin*, one of the messengers in the body's nervous system known to have a calming effect, acting as a mild tranquillizer. Avoid protein; it gets in the way and makes more tyrosine available to your brain when you least need it. Fats add to the calming effect of food, but are harder to digest and stay longer in your system: they can give you the risk of night-time heartburn to disturb sleep.

Carbohydrates to help you become drowsy

- Starches: biscuits, breads, cake, chapatis, cookies, crackers, muffins, pastas, pies, rolls, scones and tortillas.
- Sugars: confectionery and candy, honey, ice cream, jams, jellies, table sugar and syrup.
- Fruits: apples, bananas, melons, oranges, peaches, pears.
- Vegetables: carrots, corn-on-the-cob, potatoes, rice and sweet potatoes.

Meal strategies

Before placing your order for a meal, study the menu to be sure you know the ingredients of the dishes being offered and how they are prepared. If you are uncertain, ask the waiter to explain the contents of an item. In Japan, wax replicas of dishes are displayed in restaurant windows; in countries such as Greece, you can visit the restaurant kitchen and point to what you want.

Avoid rich or high-fat menu items that are described as *au gratin*, breaded, buttered or buttery, fried (batter fried, deep fried, or french fried), with cheese sauce, creamy or in a cream sauce, with hollandaise, in pan gravy, or scalloped.

For breakfast

To get off to a good start at the beginning of your daytime-active phase after a long flight, have a hearty high-protein, low-fat breakfast. Don't skip it. There's a lot to be said for a good English breakfast—so long as it's not fried. For instance, choose a two-egg omelette, two poached eggs, or a small piece of lean grilled ham, with wholegrain bread toast lightly-buttered or spread thinly with a meat extract. Forgo marmalade, jam or honey on your toast, and don't put sugar or honey in your tea or coffee, although sugar-free substitutes are fine. In Japan, you can order fish for breakfast or have a Western-style meal in hotels. In India, although people usually eat breads or rice-based dishes at this time of the day, hotels will serve a cooked meal of meats and eggs.

A 'continental breakfast' such as croissants, rolls and jam, all high in carbohydrates, overloads your blood sugar to make it go into a steep decline within an hour. You're doomed to sleepiness for the remainder of the morning. But you don't have to give up sweet goodies—starchy high-fat foods such as fried doughnuts, pastries or pancakes drizzled with syrup, which tend to make you sag during the morning, can be a treat later in the day when you *want* to become drowsy.

Many people say they never eat breakfast. If you aren't used to having a meal at that time, at least have either a glass of skimmed milk, some low-fat yogurt, a plain boiled egg, or a wedge of cheese to give yourself a shot of protein.

For lunch

Eating protein foods sustains your level of energy and fights off the early afternoon slump when alertness takes a dip: chicken or tuna salad, tossed with minimum dressing, a small lean beefburger (without the bun), a small bowl of chili con carne, or some low-fat cottage cheese. In India, curried lamb, chicken or fish is popular at lunch-time.

For dinner

Enjoy a bowl of vegetable soup, a plate of steaming noodles or spaghetti (without the meat sauce), pasta salads, crêpes (with no meat filling), a baked potato with a topping of Mexican salsa, vegetable ravioli, risotti (rice casseroles), vegetarian dishes (with no meat, cheese or eggs), a plate of steamed vegetables, or a green salad served with crusty wholegrain bread. Dinner in the Orient can be noodle soups, vegetables, steamed rice and vegetable-filled dumplings. (If your destination is a country where food may be contaminated, avoid unpeeled fruits, raw salads and uncooked vegetables.)

Evening snacks can be a couple of sweet biscuits, a small Vegemite sandwich or a piece of fruit, with herbal tea and honey or sugar. Honey helps calm you down and promotes sleep; it's metabolized faster than table sugar, giving an even greater sugar rush. (Artificial sweeteners, however, such as aspartame ('Nutrasweet') do *not* affect brain chemistry to induce drowsiness.)

Go easy on portions! The experienced jet-traveller eats frugally, taking only small portions, without overloading. Large meals may make you sleepy, but can disrupt your sleep cycle by keeping your digestive system working overtime when it is trying to adjust.

Milk is always good food. But does it give the traveller alertness or sleepiness? The answer is that the nutrients in milk have pluses and minuses. A glass of skimmed milk (about 8 fl.oz/240ml) stimulates brain chemicals and stirs up mental energy. It provides tyrosine to the brain, helping you to think faster and more accurately, making it good to take in the early part of the day. On the other hand, a glass of warm milk used to be recommended for sound sleep. It provides calcium which some say has a sleep-inducing effect. Milk also has tryptophan, but only a tiny amount which may be insufficient to induce sleep. In theory, milk's high-protein content tends to block the tryptophan from reaching your brain—but if you find that a glass of warm milk is comforting at the end of the day and helpful when you need sleep, drink it.

Indigestion and Constipation

Inactivity, prolonged sitting on the plane, irregular or unusual meals, overeating and travel stress—they are all situations that can create a medley of problems for your digestive system and bring it to a virtual halt, while your internal clocks are spinning in confusion. A basic rule is to eat lightly; small portions of food can generally be better tolerated.

Gas can be a problem when flying. It's natural to have some gas in your digestive system, but it expands as atmospheric pressure is reduced, at higher altitudes. You want to minimize the amount of gas inside you: avoid foods that form gases (beans, cabbage, onions, for instance), fatty, greasy foods, anything deep-fried, and carbonated drinks. Eat slowly to reduce the amount of air you swallow. Gas problems brought on by altitude should disappear shortly after you land. Just eat less for two days after landing, to allow the stomach to contract from gas expansion. Avoid taking high doses of antacids containing aluminium; they have been linked with poor quality sleep, and could increase jet-lag insomnia.

If you are an ulcer patient, talk to your doctor before travel. You probably are already warned off coffee, alcohol and smoking; follow your doctor's instructions regarding a special diet. Milk is no longer considered the friend of an ulcer patient, since the fat content can trigger acid production.

You may be prone to constipation when you travel—millions of travellers are. It helps to drink more water and exercise whenever you have the chance during the trip. For suppers, light dinners and evening snacks, make your high-carbohydrate meals high-fibre too. Increase your servings of wholegrain breads and cereals, bran cereals, green and yellow vegetables, plenty of fresh fruit, fruit salads and stewed prunes. When you leave home, clear the refrigerator of fresh fruit to take with you, and buy wholemeal scones (bran muffins) at local bakeries for evening snacks.

If you still need help, a soluble-fibre laxative can regulate your digestive system without jolting it into action, and can help reset the gastric clock. (For more about coping with indigestion and constipation, see the author's *The Complete Guide to Digestive Health*, Thorsons 1990.)

Drinks

Water

Drink plenty of liquids while flying and after you land. The air-conditioning in aircraft cabins makes the air extremely dry, with humidity sometimes as low as 2 per cent, and during a long flight your body becomes dehydrated. Dehydration aggravates jet lag, and tiredness causes dryness of mouth, throat, eyes and skin. Drinking water is vital to digestion and metabolism; it carries nutrients and oxygen to cells through the blood, flushes out toxins, relieves constipation, and prevents fluid/water retention. If you drink insufficient water, your body starts retaining it to compensate for the shortage, causing puffy feet and ankles during flight; to avoid fluid retention you need to drink *more*, not less (unless your doctor has ruled otherwise). As a rule of thumb, drink a glass of water or pure fruit juice every hour you are travelling. Don't wait until you are thirsty: thirst is not a reliable guide to your body's fluid balance. If you are doubtful about the safety of the water at your destination, boil it, treat it with purification tablets, or drink bottled water or mineral water (without natural or added effervescence).

Juices and soft drinks

Stick to orange, pineapple, grapefruit or apple juice; tomato juice is most likely to contain salt and would put too much sodium into your system, producing unwanted water retention. Avoid soft drinks that are carbonated, effervescent or fizzy; the bubbles increase in size in your stomach during flight, creating heartburn and indigestion.

Coffee, tea, chocolate and cola drinks

These four are the most common beverages in the world, and fortunately they contain natural chemicals that can help you successfully beat jet lag. Tea contains the chemicals *theophylline* and *caffeine,* coffee and chocolate contain the naturally-occurring chemicals *theobromine* and caffeine; most cola drinks also have caffeine.

These three chemicals are in a major category called *methylated xanthines* found in more than sixty species of plants, and which have an amazing ability to reset body clocks and reduce jet-lag symptoms. They can affect billions of body cells to change to new time zones, cutting off days of jet-lag suffering. The jet-setter can literally 'turn back the clock', using two cups of strong coffee in the *morning* when flying *west*, to adjust body clocks to an earlier hour. Two cups of strong coffee in the *evening* when travelling *east* can turn inner clocks to a later hour. An afternoon cup appears to make scarcely any change—so your four o'clock tea is not in jeopardy!

The trick is to reserve the methylated xanthines for only the times *when you need them* in the Beat Jet Lag Plans. The time to take them will vary according to the direction you are travelling, the number of time zones you are crossing, and the time you arrive at your destination. If you're a heavy coffee drinker or strong-tea fiend, your body may have developed a tolerance for caffeine, and you won't get much of a boost. The methylated xanthines will work best if you stop having these drinks one to three days before your trip, depending on the number of zones crossed, and then carefully follow the Beat Jet Lag Plan for the right time to use them to jolt your clocks. Don't rush to resume your usual coffee- and tea-drinking after landing; you'll only confuse your clock systems.

How does caffeine work?

It stimulates the central nervous system, and can increase body temperature, increase your heartbeat, speed up kidney function and metabolism, dilate certain blood vessels, and constrict others. It can improve concentration, mood and alertness, and increase muscle capacity. Caffeine can give you a 'lift', help you feel wide awake, and ready to focus on mental and physical tasks such as driving.

Caffeine occurs in drinks such as coffee (regular, decaffeinated and acid-neutralized), coffee liqueurs, tea, some herbal teas, drinking chocolate, cocoa, chocolate cordials, many soft drinks, and in coffee- or chocolate-flavoured biscuits, cakes, ice creams, jellies, puddings and sweets. Caffeine also occurs naturally in maté tea (made from *Ilex paraguariensis*), popular in South America and available in health-food shops.

Although you can probably count the cups of tea or coffee downed each day, it's nearly impossible to keep track of the caffeine in every food and drug, as the government doesn't require naturally-occurring caffeine to be shown on food labels. However, the Caffeine Scorecard in Figure 4 gives the approximate amount of caffeine in some of the most common drinks, foods, diet aids and medicines.

Item	Quantity	Caffeine
Coffee:		(mg)
Brewed: drip method	5fl.oz/150ml	60-180
percolated	5fl.oz/150ml	40-170
Instant	5fl.oz/150ml	30-120
Decaffeinated: brewed	5fl.oz/150ml	2-5
instant	5fl.oz/150ml	1-5
Tea:		
Brewed: 1 minute	5fl.oz/150ml	9-33
3 minutes	5fl.oz/150ml	20-46
5 minutes	5fl.oz/150ml	20-50
Instant	5fl.oz/150ml	25-50
Decaffeinated	5fl.oz/150ml	10-40
Iced tea	12fl.oz/355ml	67-76
Cocoa and chocolate:		
Cocoa beverage	5fl.oz/150ml	2-20
Chocolate milk beverage	8fl.oz/240ml	2-7
Chocolate-flavoured syrup	1oz/28g	4
Baking chocolate	1oz/28g	26
Dark chocolate	1oz/28g	5-35
Soft drinks:		
Coca-Cola	12fl.oz/355ml	46
Diet Coke	12fl.oz/355ml	46
Pepsi-Cola	12fl.oz/355ml	38

Item	Quantity	Caffeine
		(mg)
Diet Pepsi	12fl.oz/355ml	36
Nonprescription drugs:		
Alertness tablets:		
Nodoz	standard dose	100
Vivarin	standard dose	200
Cold remedies:		
Coryban-D capsules	standard dose	30
Dristan	standard dose	32
Triaminicin	standard dose	30
Diuretics:		
Aqua-Ban	standard dose	100
Maximum Strength		
Aqua-Ban Plus	standard dose	200
Permathene H2 Off	standard dose	200
Pre-Mens Forte	standard dose	100
Pain relievers:		
Plain aspirin	standard dose	—
Anacin	standard dose	64
Midol	standard dose	65
Excedrin	standard dose	130
Weight-control aids:		
Dexatrim	daily dose	200
Dietac capsules	daily dose	200
Prolamine	daily dose	280
Prescription drugs:		
For migraine:		
Cafergot	standard dose	100
For tension headaches:		
Fiorinal	standard dose	40
For pain relief:		
Darvon	standard dose	32

(Source: U.S. Food and Drug Administration, Food Additive Chemistry Evaluation Branch and National Center for Drugs and Biologics; the National Soft Drink Association, Washington, DC, 1983; *Consumer Reports*, January 1986.)

Figure 4: Caffeine Scorecard

A word of caution: people vary with their response to caffeine. Any change in coffee-drinking habits—either more or less than usual—can trigger a headache. If you don't drink much coffee, you may be sensitive to as little as 200 milligrams of caffeine; and most people suffer sleeplessness after about 250 milligrams. Check with your doctor if you have medical problems or aren't used to caffeine-containing drinks. Large amounts can inflame and irritate the digestive tract, increase ulcer symptoms, increase stomach acid, cause diarrhoea and increase jitteriness. Caffeine can produce dehydration (so you don't want to have any while you're on the plane). Caffeine is generally not recommended if you are pregnant (or think you may be) because of the danger of birth defects, and is not advisable for heart patients. You can still beat jet lag by following the light exposure and food recommendations in this guide.

Coffee

The amount of caffeine in a cup of coffee depends on your personal taste and preference; you may like coffee strong or weak. In the Middle East and Indonesia, for instance, people prefer very strong coffee; Americans usually drink it much milder. Caffeine content is influenced by the variety of bean, where it was grown, particle size (coffee grind) and the method used for brewing, which varies from country to country.

Tea

The amount of caffeine and theophylline in tea (from *Camellia sinensis*) depends on where the tea was grown, the variety of tea, the tea-leaf cut, the method you use for steeping and how strong you prefer your tea. The length of steeping time determines, and increases, the strength of the caffeine. Loose teas generally contain less caffeine than their brand-mates in bags. Decaffeinated tea may still contain up to 40 milligrams of caffeine, depending on the brand. Some specialty teas flavoured with spices, mint or nuts may contain caffeine not only from tea leaves but also the leaves of South American maté.

Herbal teas

Most herbal teas are caffeine-free, but as they can come from a variety of plants that have not been fully evaluated, they may contain stimulants other than caffeine and their effect on inner body clocks is not yet known.

Chocolate

Cocoa and chocolate from cacao beans (*Theobroma cacao*) contain two related chemicals, theobromine and caffeine in the ratio of about 10 to 1. Theobromine doesn't stimulate the nervous system as much as caffeine does. Unsweetened baking chocolate is a more concentrated source of caffeine.

Cola drinks

Many soft drinks (including the diet styles) are flavoured with cola, produced from cola nuts (*Cola acuminata*), another source of caffeine. However, because an average 12-ounce (355ml) regular cola drink contains the equivalent of about 1½ ounces (40g) of sugar, this high proportion of sugar offsets the caffeine 'lift'. Read can labels, and check this table:

Drinks	**Contents**	**Use**
Diet colas	Caffeine, but *no* sugar	When caffeine is specified in the Plan (Chapter 6).
Regular colas	Caffeine *and* sugar	No time.
Non-colas	*No* caffeine, but *with* sugar	When caffeine-free alternatives are specified in the Plan, in afternoon or evening only.
Diet non-colas	*No* caffeine, *no* sugar	Any time, but having no effect on body clocks.

Drugs and medicines

Caffeine is an ingredient in more than 1000 non-prescription medicines as well as numerous prescription drugs. Most often it is found in weight-control remedies, alertness or stay-awake tablets, headache and pain-relief remedies, allergy medicines, cold products and diuretics (urine-inducing medicine). Caffeine may be part of prescriptions for migraine headaches, tension headaches and muscle relaxants. If you need to take several medications, you may have more caffeine from drug sources than from your diet; the tossing and turning during the night could be the result of the painkiller taken before bedtime.

Consult your doctor concerning the medicines you take regularly. Altering or discontinuing your dosage could be unsafe, without your physician's advice.

Caffeine-free alternatives

When the Plans specify caffeine-free drinks and you *don't* want caffeine, choose from the following alternatives.

- grain-based drinks such as Aromalt, Barleycup, Caro, and Prewett's Instant Chicory (or in the United States, look for Caffix, Postum and Pero)
- caffeine-free non-carbonated soft drinks, fruit drinks and juices
- hot water with a squeeze of lemon juice
- commercial herb teas (be sure they are caffeine-free)
- bouillon made from vegetable extracts
- miso broth
- soya milk

Alcohol
When you're on the plane, alcohol may be more of a temptation than elsewhere because you feel stressed, have nothing much else to do, the drinks are cheap or sometimes free, and the small bottles don't seem to hold much. But whatever your capacity for cocktails, alcohol and altitude don't mix, and you are much better off if you skip it while flying.

There's no doubt that flying at high altitude increases thirst, but three gin and tonics or martinis in the air equal four on the ground. In the air, alcohol is far more dangerous because it interferes with your body's ability to process oxygen, and can make you feel elevated to 10 000 feet. Like caffeine, alcohol acts as a diuretic, making you even more dehydrated, which is not what you want in the bone-dry atmosphere of the jet. While an occasional drink can be pleasant, overdoing it depresses the central nervous system in a similar way to barbiturates, tranquillizers and anaesthetics, and dulls the senses, slowing your reaction time and readjustment. Although alcohol can make you drowsy, it causes fragmented less-restful sleep by reducing the amount of REM (rapid eye movement) sleep. (See **What is Sleep?** in Chapter 7.) That, in turn, cuts down concentration, decreases memory, and makes you tired and irritable.

If you absolutely can't do without a drink: during a *westbound* flight, have a glass of wine or a wine-cooler, preferably when the meal is served. On an *eastbound* flight, don't drink alcohol at all since it slows the free-running clock. And don't drink alcohol if you are taking any medicines, particularly sleeping pills.

CHAPTER 6

BEAT JET LAG PLANS

Maybe you're thinking: "Theory is fine, but I want details of exactly what to do on my next trip." So the Beat Jet Lag Plans will tell you the right time for:

- using light
- using the right foods
- using caffeine
- mental activity and social interaction
- exercise

The major recommendations of the previous chapters are coordinated here and tailored to twelve individual programmes:

> **PLAN 2 EAST** and **PLAN 2 WEST**, for 1, 1½, 2 and 2½ time zones
> **PLAN 4 EAST** and **PLAN 4 WEST**, for 3, 3½, 4 and 4½ time zones
> **PLAN 6 EAST** and **PLAN 6 WEST**, for 5, 5½, 6 and 6½ time zones
> **PLAN 8 EAST** and **PLAN 8 WEST**, for 7, 7½, 8 and 8½ time zones
> **PLAN 10 EAST** and **PLAN 10 WEST**, for 9, 9½, 10 and 10½ time zones
> **PLAN 12 EAST** and **PLAN 12 WEST**, for 11, 11½, 12 and 12½ time zones

If you are travelling more than twelve time zones in the same direction, refer to the Plan for travel in the opposite direction. For instance, for *fourteen* zones east, refer to Plan 10 west; for *sixteen* zones west, refer to Plan 8 east.

How the Plans work

Each Plan has three main steps: Before flight, Flight day and After flight, with specific recommendations for sleeping, eating, drinking methylated xanthines, preferred times for departure and arrival, light exposure, and time to be allowed before important appointments.

How many time zones are you crossing?

For a quick reference to the number of zones from London, refer to Appendix 1; from New York, refer to Appendix 2; from Sydney, refer to Appendix 3. For time differences between other major cities, refer to Appendix 4.

In theory, each time-zone strip should be about 1600 kilometres (1000 miles) wide (fifteen degrees of longitude) at the Equator and taper to each pole. In practice, the boundaries have a few zigzags and detours to make it easier for countries united politically or economically. Note that China, which stretches across fifty degrees of longitude, officially uses only one single time, so that clocks across the whole country conform to Beijing time.

When calculating the number of zones you are crossing, remember you might need to allow for 'Summer Time' (Daylight Saving Time). The actual dates in spring and autumn are fixed by individual countries and can change from year to year, so it's best to check with your travel agent. When countries in the Southern Hemisphere observe this time-shift, it will be effective during *their* summertime (wintertime in the Northern Hemisphere). The USSR advances clocks by one hour year-round, in a permanent Daylight Saving time-shift.

Crossing the International Date Line out in the Pacific Ocean, going westward you 'lose' a day; going eastward you repeat one day on the calendar. This change doesn't affect jet lag, but can sometimes add to travel confusion.

Flying time

Each Plan gives a few examples of flights crossing that range of time zones; flying time is the number of hours for a normal commercial flight, including any necessary fuel stops at intermediate airports but excluding any extended layovers.

If your plane is delayed taking off or landing, or if you have an unscheduled layover, keep to the destination sleep/wake/meals timing as much as possible.

Light exposure

Each Plan details your best time for exposure to daylight or bright indoor light, to speed resetting of body clocks, depending on the direction of your flight. Travelling midwinter or midsummer across the Equator, daylight conditions can go from one extreme to the other, making the timing of your light exposure most important.

Food and drink

Each Plan tells you the best time to take a clock-resetting dose of the methylated xanthines (coffee, tea, cocoa, or cola drinks), and when to avoid them, and gives the composition of meals suggested in Chapter 5.

For meals during the flight, ask your travel agent or airline office when meals will be served and the food selections. Airlines usually offer choices of meals, depending on diet and religion (such as vegetarian, kosher, low-fat, low-sodium, low-cholesterol). When booking the flight, put in your request for high-protein low-fat breakfasts and lunches and high-carbohydrate dinners.

Time Allowance

Even though the Beat Jet Lag Plans are effective, and will successfully reduce the time to readjust to a new zone, it takes a few days to produce results after flights across several zones. Consequently, each Plan has a time allowance, depending on the number of zones crossed, of the days to recuperate before an important appointment, engagement, athletic competition or the start of a hectic sightseeing tour. Each day you allow yourself will bring an increase in energy, concentration, and fresh alertness. When you schedule first appointments after arrival, your best physical and mental performance will be in the afternoon or the morning, depending on whether the direction of the flight was eastward or westward.

Plan 2 East

Eastbound flight

Watch advanced 2 hours

Flight examples:	Number of time zones:	Flying time: (hours)
Delhi to Hong Kong	2½	5.15
Lima to Sao Paulo	2	4.45
London to Johannesburg	2	11.30
New York to Rio de Janeiro	2	9.15
Perth to Adelaide	1½	2.45
Seattle to Dallas	2	3.45

This Plan is devised for eastbound 1, 1½, 2 and 2½ time-zone changes. (The Plan could also be followed for a nonstop westbound flight crossing twenty-two time zones—although that is *not* a preferred itinerary.)

Each spring we have a 'time-zone change' of one hour when clocks are advanced with the beginning of Daylight Saving Time/Summer Time. Travelling across one or two time zones may not put your body clocks into as great a whirl as trips that involve many time-shifts; nevertheless, jet-lag symptoms can still be tiredness, lack of appetite, constipation or indigestion and confusion. By following each step in the Beat Jet Lag Plan, you can quickly be in step with your new time frame. The times for light exposure after landing are especially important.

Before flight
Sleep
The day before you fly, go to bed and get up one or two hours earlier than usual.

Drinks
For two days before you fly, stop drinking coffee, tea, cocoa, chocolate or cola drinks with caffeine, and avoid caffeine-containing drugs and diet aids. Switch to the caffeine-free beverages listed in Chapter 5. If you find it impossible to go without your usual uplifting cup, at least make it very weak, and drink it only at about 4.00 p.m. The day before you fly, between 7.00 p.m. and 11.00 p.m., take two cups of strong black coffee or tea (no cream or sugar, although sugar-free sweeteners are allowed).

Meals
On the day before flight, eat lightly, with mealtimes according to destination time: a high-protein, low-fat breakfast and lunch, and a high-

carbohydrate supper, as outlined in Chapter 5. No evening snack.

Flight day
(With a 2-hour time-shift, this day has only 22 hours)

Best departure and arrival times
For a short flight, depart early in the day. For a long flight, have an early departure, on a day flight, with arrival before midnight; *or* a late departure before midnight, on a night flight, with arrival the next day after 6.00 a.m. destination time.

Time change
Immediately you board the aircraft, advance your watch to the time at today's destination. Forget the old time zone, and focus on what you will be doing after your flight.

Sleep
Rise one or two hours earlier than usual. When you arrive, sleep on destination time. Because 11.00 p.m. destination time would be 9.00 p.m. in the old zone, you may not feel tired, but get to bed, keep your eyes closed or use an eye-mask, and relax.

Drinks
Take no coffee, tea, cocoa, chocolate or cola drinks containing caffeine today, or caffeine-containing drugs and diet aids. Use caffeine-free beverages. During the flight, drink plenty of water or fruit juices to counteract aircraft dehydration. Avoid alcohol, or limit yourself to only one drink with a meal.

Meals
Eat lightly, with mealtimes according to destination time. Eat a high-protein, low-fat breakfast and lunch, and a high-carbohydrate supper, but no evening snack.

After flight
Sleep
Go to bed and wake up according to local time. Set your alarm clock, or ask the hotel staff for a prompt wake-up call, so you don't oversleep. Then rise and shine! Immediately turn on lively radio, television or video.

Do the Energizing Exercises in Chapter 4 to rouse your body and brain. Go to bed at 11.00 p.m. local time even if you are not tired (it would be 9.00 p.m. in the old time zone), to relax and prepare yourself for sleep. Chapter 7 gives ways to counteract insomnia and induce sleep.

Light
Be outdoors and active, 6.00 a.m. to 8.00 a.m. If there is no daylight outdoors, be near bright indoor light.

Drinks
No caffeine drinks today. To help your digestive clock and avert constipation, continue drinking plenty of water (at least eight glasses a day), starting with a glass of water when you wake and a glass before each meal.

Meals
Eat lightly, according to local time, with high-protein, low-fat breakfasts and lunches, and high-carbohydrate suppers. To avoid constipation, suppers and evening snacks should include fruit (such as apples, pears, stewed prunes or figs), vegetables, wholegrain breads and high-fibre cereals.

Time Allowance
For best mental and physical activity, and before the start of tours:
—with the Beat Jet Lag Plan, none is necessary
—without the Beat Jet Lag Plan, none is necessary.
Schedule first appointments and activities during the afternoons.

Plan 2 West

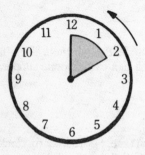

Watch set back 2 hours   Westbound flight

Flight examples:	Number of time zones:	Flying time: (hours)
Auckland to Sydney	2	3.30
Bangkok to Delhi	1½	4.00
Bombay to Nairobi	2½	6.00
Cape Town to London	2	13.45
Chicago to Las Vegas	2	3.45
Perth to Bangkok	1	6.45

This Plan is devised for westbound 1, 1½, 2 and 2½ time-zone changes. (The Plan could also be followed for a nonstop eastbound flight crossing twenty-two time zones—although that is *not* a preferred itinerary.)

Every autumn, when clocks are set back an hour at the end of Daylight Saving Time/Summer Time, we have the effect of a one-hour 'time-zone change'. Flying west and crossing two time zones doesn't appear to be as troublesome to most people as crossing two time zones east, and we can usually adjust more quickly to an expanded day rather than a condensed day because of the body's natural desire to follow a sleep/wake cycle of about twenty-five hours.

Length of flight can be a factor in tiredness: for instance, flying from New York to Mexico City is crossing only one time zone but several thousand miles. You will be tired at the end of the journey, but you shouldn't be suffering the worst symptoms of jet lag. However, the Beat Jet Lag Plan will effectively reset your inner clocks and get you in step with your destination. Carefully follow the specified times for light exposure after landing.

Before flight
Sleep
For two days before you fly, get up and go to bed one or two hours later than usual.

Drinks
For two days before flight, stop drinking coffee, tea, cocoa, chocolate or cola drinks with caffeine, and avoid caffeine-containing drugs and diet aids. Switch to the caffeine-free beverages listed in Chapter 5. If you find it impossible to go without your usual uplifting cup, at least make it very weak and drink it only at about 4.00 p.m.

Meals
On the day before you fly, eat a high-protein, low-fat breakfast and lunch, and a high-carbohydrate dinner, according to Chapter 5.

Flight day
(With a 2-hour time-shift, this day has 26 hours)

Best departure and arrival times
For a short flight, depart early afternoon. For a long flight, choose one that arrives during your normal active phase, about 4.00 p.m. destination time.

Time change
Immediately you board the aircraft, set your watch back to the time at today's destination. Forget the old time zone, and focus on what you'll be doing after your flight.

Sleep
Rise one or two hours later than usual. After landing, sleep on destination time. Because 11.00 p.m. destination time would be 1.00 a.m. in the old zone, you may want to go to bed early.

Drinks
Take two cups of strong black coffee or tea in the morning *only,* between 7.00 a.m. and 11.00 a.m. (no cream or sugar, although sugar-free sweeteners are allowed). During the flight, drink plenty of water or fruit juices to counteract aircraft dehydration. Avoid alcohol, or limit yourself to just one drink with a meal.

Meals
Eat lightly, with mealtimes according to destination time. Eat a high-protein, low-fat breakfast and lunch, a high-carbohydrate dinner and, perhaps, an evening snack of carbohydrates.

After flight
Sleep
It will be easy to wake up the morning after a flight westward. Enjoy the luxury of lying in bed until you need to rise, or get up and do chores, write reports or do exercises before breakfast. Don't nap during the day. Stay

active. If you are alone in the evening, turn on lively radio, television or
video. Sleep according to local time.

Light
Be outdoors and active: 4.00 p.m. to 6.00 p.m. If there is no daylight
outdoors at that time, be near bright indoor light.

Drinks
No caffeine drinks today. To help your digestive clock and avert
constipation, continue drinking plenty of water (at least eight glasses a
day), starting with a glass when you wake and a glass before each meal.

Meals
Eat lightly, with high-protein, low-fat breakfasts and lunches, and high-
carbohydrate dinners. Have a carbohydrate evening snack, if you wish.
To avoid constipation, dinners and late snacks should include fruit (such
as apples, pears, stewed prunes or figs), vegetables, wholegrain breads
and high-fibre cereals.

Time Allowance
For best mental and physical activity, and before the start of tours:
  —with the Beat Jet Lag Plan, none is necessary
  —without the Beat Jet Lag Plan, none is necessary.
Schedule first appointments and activities during the mornings.

Plan 4 East

Eastbound flight   Watch advanced 4 hours

Flight examples:	Number of time zones:	Flying time: (hours)
Delhi to Tokyo	3½	8.15
Hong Kong to Auckland	4	11.15
London to Dar es Salaam	3	10.45
London to Moscow	3	3.45
Paris to Bombay	4½	8.45
Riyadh to Bangkok	4	7.00

This Plan is devised for eastbound 3, 3½, 4 and 4½ time-zone changes. (The Plan could also be followed for a nonstop westbound flight crossing twenty time zones—although that is *not* a preferred itinerary.)

Crossing a continent, or flying from one continent to another, usually involves a time-zone change of about three or four hours. You may think you have a short trip, but you can still be troubled by considerable jet-lag problems if you take no countermeasures. Have confidence that the Beat Jet Lag Plan will greatly reduce symptoms and trigger your system for a fast change to the new time zone. Carefully follow the specified times for light exposure after landing.

Before flight
Sleep
For two or three days before you fly, retire to bed and get up two hours earlier than usual.

Drinks
For three days before you fly, stop drinking coffee, tea, cocoa, chocolate or cola drinks with caffeine, and avoid caffeine-containing drugs and diet aids. Switch to the caffeine-free beverages listed in Chapter 5. If you find it impossible to go without your usual uplifting cup, at least make it weak, and drink it only at about 4.00 p.m.

Meals
On the day before you fly, have mealtimes two hours earlier than usual and take only small portions. Eat a high-protein, low-fat breakfast and lunch, and high-carbohydrate supper, according to Chapter 5.

Flight day
(With a 4-hour time-shift, this day has only 20 hours)

Best departure and arrival times
For a short flight, depart early in the day. For a long flight, have an early departure, on a day flight, with arrival before midnight; *or* a late departure before midnight, on a night flight, with arrival the next day after 6.00 a.m. destination time.

Time change
Immediately you board the aircraft, advance your watch to the time at today's destination. Forget the old time zone, and focus on what you'll be doing after your flight.

Sleep
Rise two hours earlier than usual. After landing, sleep on destination time, if possible. If you generally go to bed at 11.00 p.m., it would be only 7.00 p.m. in the old zone, so you may not feel tired. However, it's important to get to bed and prepare yourself for sleep, keep your eyes closed or use an eye-mask, and relax.

Drinks
No coffee, tea, cocoa, chocolate or cola drinks containing caffeine in the morning or afternoon, or caffeine-containing drugs and diet aids. Use caffeine-free beverages. Then between 7.00 p.m. and 11.00 p.m. old time zone (wherever you may be), take two cups of strong black coffee or tea (no cream or sugar, although sugar-free sweeteners are allowed). During the flight, drink plenty of water or fruit juices to counteract aircraft dehydration. Avoid alcohol, or limit yourself to only one drink with a meal.

Meals
Eat lightly, with mealtimes according to destination time. Have a high-protein, low-fat breakfast and lunch, and a high-carbohydrate supper; no evening snack.

After flight
Sleep
Go to bed and wake up according to local time. Set your alarm clock, or ask the hotel staff for a prompt wake-up call, so you don't oversleep. Then rise and shine! Immediately turn on lively radio, television or video. Do the Energizing Exercises in Chapter 4 to rouse your body and brain. No napping during the day. Stay active. Retire to bed at 11.00 p.m. local time, even if you are not tired, to relax and prepare yourself for sleep.

Chapter 7 gives ways to counteract insomnia and induce sleep.

Light
Be outdoors and active: 6.00 a.m. to 10.00 a.m. If there is no daylight outdoors, be near bright indoor light.

Drinks
No caffeine drinks today. To help the digestive clock and avoid constipation, continue drinking plenty of water (at least eight glasses a day), starting with a glass when you wake and a glass before each meal.

Meals
Eat lightly, with mealtimes on local time. Have high-protein breakfasts and lunches. Your high-carbohydrate suppers should include fruit (such as apples, pears, stewed prunes or figs), vegetables, wholegrain breads and high-fibre cereals, to keep your digestive system running smoothly. If constipation remains a problem, correct it gently with a soluble-fibre laxative.

Time Allowance
For best mental and physical activity, and before the start of tours:
   —with the Beat Jet Lag Plan, none is necessary
   —without the Beat Jet Lag Plan, allow one to two days.
After your time allowance, schedule first appointments and activities in the afternoons.

Plan 4 West

Watch set back 4 hours   Westbound flight

Flight examples:	Number of time zones:	Flying time: (hours)
Atlanta to Seattle	3	5.15
Auckland to Perth	4	7.15
Dar es Salaam to London	3	10.45
Delhi to Frankfurt	4½	8.30
London to Rio de Janeiro	3	11.30
Santiago to Los Angeles	4	16.30

This Plan is devised for westbound 3, 3½, 4 and 4½ time-zone changes. (The Plan could also be followed for a nonstop eastbound flight crossing twenty time zones—although that is *not* a preferred itinerary.)

Crossing three or four time zones to the west can bring uncomfortable jet-lag symptoms of indigestion, constipation and out-of-phase sleeping and waking—although not as severe as crossing the same number of zones going east. However, the Beat Jet Lag Plan will help you rapidly reset your inner clocks and give you a successful trip. The times for light exposure after landing are especially important.

Before flight
Sleep
For three days before you fly, get up and go to bed two hours later than usual.

Drinks
For three days before the flight, stop drinking coffee, tea, cocoa, chocolate or cola drinks with caffeine, and avoid caffeine-containing drugs and diet aids. Switch to the caffeine-free beverages listed in Chapter 5. If you find it impossible to go without your usual uplifting cup, at least make it weak and drink it only at about 4.00 p.m.

Meals
On the day before you fly, try to make mealtimes an hour or two later than usual. Eat a high-protein, low-fat breakfast and lunch, and a high-carbohydrate dinner, as outlined in Chapter 5.

Flight day
(With a 4-hour time-shift, this day has 28 hours)

Best departure and arrival times

For a short flight, depart early afternoon. For a long flight, choose one that arrives during your normal active phase, about 4.00 p.m. destination time.

Time change

Immediately you board the aircraft, set your watch back to the time at today's destination. Forget the old time zone, and focus on what you'll be doing after your flight.

Sleep

Give yourself the luxury of rising two hours later than usual. Avoid napping during the day, and stay active. Sleep tonight on destination time, if possible. You may feel tired early; if you go to bed at 10.00 p.m. destination time, it would be 2.00 a.m. in the old time zone.

Drinks

Take two cups of strong black coffee or tea in the morning *only*, between 7.00 a.m. and 11.00 a.m. (no cream or sugar, although sugar-free sweeteners are allowed). During the flight, drink plenty of water or fruit juices to counteract aircraft dehydration. Avoid alcohol, or limit yourself to just one drink with a meal.

Meals

Eat lightly, with mealtimes according to the time at today's destination. Eat a high-protein, low-fat breakfast and lunch, and a high-carbohydrate dinner—and a carbohydrate evening snack, if you like.

After flight

Sleep

Your body will want you to wake up early, after a flight westward, but you must resist the urge to rise. Stay in bed with eyes closed, enjoying the luxury of lying in bed until breakfast on local time. Don't nap during the day. Stay active. If you are alone in the evening, turn on lively radio, television or video. Sleep according to local time.

Light

Be outdoors and active: 2.00 p.m. to 6.00 p.m. If there is no daylight outdoors at those hours, be near bright indoor light.

Drinks

No caffeine drinks today. To help your digestive clock and avoid constipation, continue drinking plenty of water (at least eight glasses a day), starting with a glass when you wake and a glass before each meal.

Meals

Eat lightly, with mealtimes on local time. Have high-protein, low-fat breakfasts and lunches, and high-carbohydrate dinners. Have carbohydrate evening snacks if you like. Dinners and late snacks should include fruit (apples, pears, stewed prunes), vegetables, wholegrain breads and high-fibre cereals, to keep your digestive system running smoothly. If constipation remains a problem, correct it gently with a soluble-fibre laxative.

Time Allowance

For best mental and physical activity, and before the start of tours:
   —with the Beat Jet Lag Plan, none is necessary
   —without the Beat Jet Lag Plan, allow one to two days.
After your time allowance, schedule first appointments and activities during the mornings.

Plan 6 East

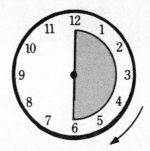

Eastbound flight   Watch advanced 6 hours

This Plan is devised for eastbound 5, 5½, 6 and 6½ time-zone changes. (The Plan could also be followed for a nonstop westbound flight crossing eighteen time zones—although that is *not* a preferred itinerary.)

Flight examples:	Number of time zones:	Flying time: (hours)
Athens to Bangkok	5	9.15
Colombo to Auckland	6½	14.15
Dallas to London	6	9.15
London to Colombo	5½	12.15
Manila to Honolulu	6	9.45
New York to Madrid	6	7.00

Jet-lag problems can be really serious after crossing five or six time zones. Flight time can be several hours or half a day, and you could expect to have a severe jolt to your body clocks without the Beat Jet Lag Plan. However, with the scientifically-based Plan, you can minimize symptoms and adjust more quickly. Carefully follow the specified times for light exposure after landing.

Before flight
Sleep
For three days before you fly, go to bed and get up two hours earlier than usual.

Drinks
For three days before you fly, stop drinking coffee, tea, chocolate, cocoa, and cola drinks with caffeine, and avoid caffeine-containing drugs and diet aids. Switch to the caffeine-free beverages listed in Chapter 5. If you find it impossible to go without your usual uplifting cup, at least make it weak, and drink it only at about 4.00 p.m.

Meals
Two days before you fly, begin the Plan with high-protein, low-fat breakfasts and lunches, and high-carbohydrate suppers. Mealtimes should be two hours earlier than usual. Eat small portions, so as not to overburden your digestive system before flight.

Flight day
(With a 6-hour time-shift, this day has only 18 hours)

Best departure and arrival times
Choose an early departure, on a day flight, with arrival before midnight

at your destination; *or* a late departure before midnight, on a night flight, with arrival the next day after 6.00 a.m. destination time.

Time change
Immediately you board the aircraft, advance your watch to the time at today's destination. Forget the old time zone, and focus on what you'll be doing after your flight.

Sleep
Rise two hours earlier than usual. After landing, sleep on local time, if possible. If you generally go to bed at 11.00 p.m., it would be 5.00 p.m. in the old zone, and you may not feel tired. Get into bed anyway, to prepare yourself for sleep, keep your eyes closed, wear an eye-mask if you like, and relax.

Drinks
Take no caffeine-containing drinks or medicines in the morning or afternoon. Use caffeine-free beverages as detailed in Chapter 5. Then between 7.00 p.m. and 11.00 p.m. old time zone (wherever you may be), take two cups of strong black coffee or tea (no cream or sugar, although sugar-free sweeteners are allowed). As you have a long flight today, be sure to drink liquids (water or fruit juices) while flying, to offset the cabin's dry atmosphere. Avoid alcohol, or limit yourself to just one drink with a meal.

Meals
Eat lightly, with mealtimes according to your destination time. Have a high-protein, low-fat breakfast and lunch, and a high-carbohydrate evening snack only (omitting supper).

After flight
Sleep
Go to bed and wake up according to local time. Set your alarm clock, or ask the hotel staff for a prompt wake-up call, so you don't oversleep. Then rise and shine! Immediately turn on lively radio, television or video. Do the Energizing Exercises in Chapter 4 to rouse your body and brain. No napping during the day; stay active. Retire to bed about 11.00 p.m., even if you are not tired, to relax and prepare for sleep. Chapter 7 gives ways to counteract insomnia and induce sleep.

Light
Be outdoors and active: 6.00 a.m. to 12.00 noon. If there is no daylight at these hours, be near bright indoor light.

Drinks
No caffeine drinks today. To help your digestive clock and avoid constipation, continue drinking plenty of water (at least eight glasses a day), starting with a glass when you wake and a glass before each meal.

Meals
Eat lightly, with mealtimes on local time. Have high-protein, low-fat breakfasts and lunches, and high-carbohydrate suppers. Suppers should include fruit (apples, pears, stewed prunes), vegetables, wholegrain breads and high-fibre cereals, to keep your digestive system running smoothly. If constipation remains a problem, correct it gently with a soluble-fibre laxative.

Time Allowance
For best mental and physical activity, and before the start of tours:
   —with the Beat Jet Lag Plan, allow one day
   —without the Beat Jet Lag Plan, allow three to six days.
After your time allowance, schedule first appointments and activities during the afternoons.

Plan 6 West

Watch set back 6 hours

Westbound flight

Flight examples:	Number of time zones:	Flying time: (hours)
Anchorage to Tokyo	6	7.30
Bombay to London	5½	10.30
Honolulu to Hong Kong	6	11.00
London to Mexico City	6	14.00
London to New York	5	7.30
Perth to Harare	6	10.30

This Plan is devised for westbound 5, 5½, 6 and 6½ time-zone changes. (The Plan could also be followed for a nonstop eastbound flight crossing eighteen time zones—although that is *not* a preferred itinerary.)

You demand a considerable change in your body clocks when you cross six time zones westbound: sleep/wake patterns are severely disturbed, digestion and urine function are out of sync, and you could feel disorientated and out of touch with the rest of the world. The Beat Jet Lag Plan, however, is scientifically-based and designed to help you reduce adjustment time, and be in step with your new surroundings when you arrive. Carefully follow the specified times for light exposure after landing.

Before flight
Sleep
For three days before you fly, get up and go to bed two hours later than usual. One day before you fly, make your day three hours later than usual.

Drinks
For three days before flying, stop drinking coffee, tea, cocoa, chocolate and cola drinks with caffeine, and avoid caffeine-containing drugs and diet aids. Switch to the caffeine-free alternatives listed in Chapter 5. If you find it impossible to go without your usual uplifting cup, at least make it weak, and drink it only about 4.00 p.m.

Meals
Two days before you fly, start eating high-protein, low-fat breakfasts and lunches and high-carbohydrate dinners, as outlined in Chapter 5 with mealtimes two or three hours later than usual.

Flight day
(With a 6-hour time-shift, this day has 30 hours)

Best departure and arrival times
For a short flight, depart about 12.00 noon. For a long flight, choose one that arrives during your normal active phase, about 4.00 p.m. destination time.

Time change
Immediately you board the aircraft, set your watch back to the time at today's destination. Forget the old time zone, and focus on what you'll be doing after your flight.

Sleep
Try to sleep as late as you can. After arrival, sleep on destination time, if possible. Avoid napping during the day. Stay active. You may feel tired early; if you go to bed at 9.00 p.m. at your destination, it would be 3.00 a.m. in the old zone.

Drinks
Take two cups of strong black coffee or tea in the morning *only*, between 7.00 a.m. and 11.00 a.m. (no cream or sugar, although sugar-free sweeteners are allowed). During the flight, drink plenty of water or fruit juices to counteract aircraft dehydration. Avoid alcohol, or limit yourself to just one drink with a meal.

Meals
Eat lightly, with mealtimes according to your destination time. Eat a high-protein, low-fat breakfast and lunch, a high-carbohydrate dinner and evening snack.

After flight
Sleep
After a flight westward, your body will naturally want you to wake early, but you must resist the urge to rise. Stay in bed as long as possible, keep your eyes closed and stay completely relaxed until breakfast on local time. Don't nap during the day. Stay active. If you are alone in the evening, turn on lively radio, television or video. Sleep according to local time.

Light
Be outdoors and active: 12.00 noon to 6.00 p.m. If there is no daylight outdoors at these times, be near bright indoor light.

Drinks

No caffeine drinks today. To help your digestive clock and avoid constipation, continue drinking plenty of water (at least eight glasses a day), starting with a glass when you wake and a glass before each meal.

Meals

Have your meals on local time. Eat lightly, with high-protein, low-fat breakfasts and lunches, and high-carbohydrate dinners. Have a carbohydrate evening snack, if you like. Dinners and late snacks should include fruit (such as apples, pears, stewed prunes or figs), vegetables, wholegrain breads and high-fibre cereals, to keep your digestive system running smoothly. If constipation remains a problem, correct it gently with a soluble-fibre laxative.

Time Allowance

For best mental and physical activity, and before the start of tours:
   —with the Beat Jet Lag Plan, allow one day
   —without the Beat Jet Lag Plan, allow three to four days.
After your time allowance, schedule first appointments and activities during the mornings.

Plan 8 East

Eastbound flight   Watch advanced 8 hours

Flight examples:	Number of time zones:	Flying time: (hours)
Auckland to New York	7	24.15
Brussels to Tokyo	8	17.15
Chicago to Paris	7	8.00
Delhi to Honolulu	8½	19.30
London to Perth	8	21.30
Los Angeles to London	8	10.15

This Plan is devised for eastbound 7, 7½, 8 and 8½ time-zone changes. (The Plan could also be followed for a nonstop westbound flight crossing sixteen time zones—although that is *not* a preferred itinerary.)

A time-shift of seven or eight hours eastward means that you reduce your flight day to only sixteen or seventeen hours, reducing or cutting out many hours of sleep. Loss of sleep means that when you land, it will probably be in the middle of the night 'home time' when your biological clocks are screaming at you to get to bed. A major effort is needed to collect your luggage, negotiate Passport Control and Customs, and find your way to your hotel. If you are elderly, consider breaking up the journey into sections with stopovers: with an overnight stop at an airport hotel or the sleeping rooms at major airports, you can turn a long arduous flight into two more relaxing ones. Without the Beat Jet Lag countermeasures, you could take days or even weeks to adjust, suffering daytime drowsiness and night-time insomnia. The Beat Jet Lag Plan will hasten resetting of your inner clocks to the new time zone around the globe. The times for light exposure after landing are especially important.

Before flight
Sleep
For three days before you fly, start going to bed and getting up two hours earlier each night.

Drinks
For three days before flight, stop drinking coffee, tea, chocolate, cocoa and cola drinks with caffeine, and avoid caffeine-containing drugs and diet aids. Switch to the caffeine-free beverages listed in Chapter 5. If you find it impossible to go without your usual uplifting cup, at least make it weak

and take it only at about 4.00 p.m.

Meals
Three days before you fly, start eating high-protein, low-fat breakfasts and lunches, and high-carbohydrate suppers, as outlined in Chapter 5, with mealtimes two or three hours earlier.

Flight day
(With an 8-hour time-shift, this day has only 16 hours)

Best departure and arrival times
A late afternoon or evening departure on a night flight is recommended, with arrival the next day after 6.00 a.m. destination time.

Time change
Immediately you board the aircraft, advance your watch to the time at today's destination. Forget the old time zone, and focus on what you'll be doing after your flight.

Sleep
Rise two hours earlier than usual. During the flight, sleep on destination time, if possible. If you don't feel tired, close the cabin window blinds, turn off reading lights, arrange the pillow and blanket, close your eyes or wear an eye-mask, and relax.

Drinks
No caffeine-containing drinks or medicines in the morning or afternoon. Between 7.00 p.m. and 11.00 p.m. old time zone (wherever you may be), take two cups of strong black coffee or tea (no cream or sugar, although sugar-free sweeteners are allowed). Flight times are extremely long, so remember to drink plenty of water or fruit juices during the flight, to compensate for the aircraft's low humidity and dehydrating atmosphere. Avoid alcohol during the flight, or limit yourself to one drink with a meal.

Meals
Eat lightly, with mealtimes according to destination time. Have a high-protein breakfast and lunch, and high-carbohydrate evening snack (or you may want to miss a meal, as this is a shorter day).

After flight
Sleep
If you arrive in daylight, stay active and don't nap during the day. With biological clocks reversed, sleep is heaviest in early morning local time. Set your alarm clock, or ask the hotel staff for a prompt wake-up call, so you don't oversleep. Then rise and shine! Immediately turn on lively radio, television or video. Do the Energizing Exercises in Chapter 4 to rouse your body and brain. No napping during the day; stay active. Retire to bed at 11.00 p.m. local time even if you still feel wide awake (it would be 3.00 p.m. in the old zone). Make the room dark, get into bed, close your eyes, and relax. Sleep will come. Chapter 7 gives ways to counteract insomnia and induce sleep.

Light
Remain indoors from 6.00 a.m. to 8.00 a.m., then be outdoors from 8.00 a.m. to 2.00 p.m. If there is no daylight at 8.00 a.m., be near bright indoor light.

Drinks
No caffeine drinks today. To help your digestive clock and avoid constipation, continue drinking plenty of water (at least eight glasses a day), starting with a glass when you wake and a glass before each meal.

Meals
Eat lightly, with high-protein, low-fat breakfasts and lunches, and high-carbohydrate suppers. Suppers should include fruit (apples, pears, stewed prunes and figs), vegetables, wholegrain breads and high-fibre cereals, to keep your digestive system running smoothly. If constipation remains a problem, correct it gently with a soluble-fibre laxative.

Time Allowance
For best mental and physical activity, and before the start of tours:
   —with the Beat Jet Lag Plan, allow two days
   —without the Beat Jet Lag Plan, allow five to ten days.
After your time allowance, schedule first appointments and activities in the afternoons, after 2.00 p.m.

Plan 8 West

Watch set back 8 hours

Westbound flight

Flight examples:	Number of time zones:	Flying time: (hours)
Hong Kong to London	8	13.45
London to Los Angeles	8	11.00
London to Vancouver	8	9.30
Moscow to Toronto	8	14.30
New York to Auckland	7	20.00
Tokyo to Rome	8	18.15

This Plan is devised for westbound 7, 7½, 8 and 8½ time-zone changes. (The Plan could also be followed for a nonstop eastbound flight crossing sixteen time zones—although that is *not* a preferred itinerary.)

Shooting across eight time zones to the west gives the intercontinental traveller a considerable upheaval of body clocks, whether the flight takes a whole day between Northern and Southern Hemispheres or a relatively shorter one of several hours. The disturbance may not appear to be as troublesome as flying eight zones to the east, but severe jet-lag symptoms of disrupted sleeping, waking, digestion, urine function, coordination and thought processes are all involved and can last days if not weeks. But the Beat Jet Lag Plan will effectively reduce the time needed to reset your inner clocks. Carefully follow the specified times for light exposure after landing.

Before flight
Sleep

For three days before you fly, get up and go to bed two hours later than usual. One day before you fly, make your day three hours later than usual.

Drinks

For three days before flight, stop drinking coffee, tea, cocoa, chocolate and cola drinks with caffeine, and avoid caffeine-containing drugs and diet aids. Switch to the caffeine-free beverages listed in Chapter 5. If you find it impossible to go without your usual uplifting cup, at least make it weak, and drink it only at about 4:00 p.m.

Meals

Two days before you fly, try to have mealtimes according to your destination time. Have high-protein, low-fat breakfasts and lunches and high-carbohydrate dinners, as outlined in Chapter 5. Eat small portions, so as not to burden your digestive system before the flight.

Flight day
(With an 8-hour time-shift, this day has 32 hours)

Best departure and arrival times

For a short flight, leave before noon. For a long flight, choose one that arrives during your normal active phase, about 2.00 p.m. destination time.

Time change

Immediately you board the aircraft, set your watch back to the time at today's destination. Forget the old time zone, and focus on what you'll be doing after your flight.

Sleep

Your day is going to be a long one, so try to sleep as late as possible. The early part of the flight will be the inactive phase at your destination; try to rest and relax as much as you can, to reduce the fatigue of the expanded day and the long flight. After landing, sleep on destination time, if possible. You may feel tired early; if you go to bed at 9.00 p.m. local time, it would be 5.00 a.m. in the old zone.

Drinks

Take two cups of strong black coffee or tea in the morning *only*, between 7.00 a.m. and 11.00 a.m. (no cream or sugar, but sugar-free sweeteners are allowed). During the flight, drink plenty of water or fruit juices to counteract aircraft dehydration. Avoid alcohol, or limit yourself to just one drink with a meal.

Meals

Eat lightly, with mealtimes according to the time at today's destination. Eat a high-protein, low-fat breakfast and lunch, and a high-carbohydrate dinner and evening snack.

After flight

Sleep

The morning after a westward flight, your body will naturally want you to wake early, but you must resist the urge to rise. Stay in bed as long as possible, with eyes closed, and continue complete relaxation until normal breakfast time by local clocks. Don't nap during the day; stay active. If you are alone in the evening, turn on lively radio, television or video. Sleep according to local time.

Light

Be outdoors and active from 10.00 a.m. to 4.00 p.m. If there is no daylight outdoors between those hours, be near bright indoor light. Stay indoors between 4.00 p.m. and 6.00 p.m.

Drinks

No caffeine drinks today. To help your digestive clock and avoid constipation, continue drinking plenty of water (at least eight glasses a day), starting with a glass when you wake and a glass before each meal.

Meals

Eat small portions, with mealtimes according to local time. Have high-protein, low-fat breakfasts and lunches, and high-carbohydrate dinners. Have a carbohydrate evening snack, if you like. Dinners and late snacks should include fruit (apples, pears, stewed prunes and figs), vegetables, wholegrain breads and high-fibre cereals, to keep your digestive system running smoothly. If constipation remains a problem, correct it gently with a soluble-fibre laxative.

Time Allowance
For best mental and physical activity, and before the start of tours:
   —with the Beat Jet Lag Plan, allow one day
   —without the Beat Jet Lag Plan, allow five to six days.
After your time allowance, schedule first appointments and activities
during the mornings.

Plan 10 East

Eastbound flight   Watch advanced 10 hours

Flight examples:	Number of time zones:	Flying time: (hours)
Cairo to Auckland	10	23.15
Honolulu to London	10	17.45
London to Sydney	10	22.00
London to Tokyo	9	11.45
New York to Delhi	10½	18.00
San Franciso to Paris	9	10.15

This Plan is devised for eastbound 9, 9½, 10 and 10½ time-zone changes. (The Plan could also be followed for a nonstop westbound flight crossing fourteen time zones—although that is *not* a preferred itinerary.)

    With nine or more hours of time advance, you may want to break up the journey into sections with night stopovers, especially if your flight time is a long one. Crossing polar latitudes, minimum flight time is about eight hours, but a diagonal flight such as from London to Sydney takes almost a day of flying. Whatever your flying time, you are creating a severe upheaval to your system, and a night at an airport hotel midway would make the arduous journey more relaxing.

By crossing nine or ten time zones in one leap, you are trying to turn night into day or daylight into darkness, and losing a night's sleep can make you a zombie. But when every minute counts, the Beat Jet Lag Plan devised for this time-shift will speed the radical changes you are asking your biological clocks to make, and give you a shortcut to peak performance on arrival. The times for light exposure after landing are especially important.

Before flight
Sleep
When crossing nine or more time zones, pre-adjustment of sleep time becomes preferable during two or three days prior to flight. Get up and go to bed two or three hours earlier each day. You won't fully adjust, of course, but you will have set your inner clocks in the right direction.

Drinks
For three days before your flight, stop drinking coffee, tea, chocolate, cocoa and cola drinks containing caffeine, and avoid caffeine-containing drugs and diet aids. Switch to the caffeine-free alternatives listed in Chapter 5. If you find it impossible to go without an uplifting cup, at least make it weak and take it only about 4.00 p.m.

Meals
Eat small portions and no evening snacks, so that your digestive system is not overloaded before you fly. Two or three days before, have mealtimes two or three hours earlier than usual. Start eating high-protein, low-fat breakfasts and lunches, and high-carbohydrate suppers, as detailed in Chapter 5.

Flight day
(With a 10-hour time-shift, this day has only 14 hours)

Best departure and arrival times
Late departure on a night flight is recommended, with arrival the next day after 6.00 a.m. destination time.

Time change
Immediately you board the aircraft, advance your watch to the time at

today's destination. Forget the old time zone, and focus on what you'll be doing after your flight.

Sleep
On the morning of the flight, get up two or three hours earlier than usual. During the flight, sleep if possible during what would be night time at your destination. At 11.00 p.m. destination time it would be 1.00 p.m. in the old zone; you won't feel tired, but close the cabin window blinds, turn off reading lights, arrange the pillow and blanket, close your eyes or wear an eye-mask, and relax.

Drinks
No caffeine-containing drinks or medicines in the morning or afternoon. Between 7.00 p.m. and 11.00 p.m. old time zone (wherever you may be), take two cups of strong black coffee or tea (no cream or sugar, although sugar-free sweeteners are allowed). During the flight, drink plenty of water or fruit juices to counteract the aircraft's low humidity. Avoid alcohol or limit yourself to only one drink taken with a meal.

Meals
Eat small portions, with meals according to the time at today's destination. Have a high-protein, low-fat breakfast and lunch; *no* supper or evening snack, since this is a short day.

After flight
Sleep
With a reversal of day and night, sleep comes heavily in early morning local time. Set your alarm clock or ask the hotel staff for a prompt wake-up call, so you don't oversleep. Then rise and shine! Immediately turn on lively radio, television or video. Do the Energizing Exercises in Chapter 4 to rouse your body and brain. No napping during the day. Stay active. Sleep according to local time. Retire to bed at 11.00 p.m.; you may still feel wide awake, but make the room dark, get to bed, close your eyes and relax. Chapter 7 gives ways to counteract insomnia and induce sleep.

Light
Remain indoors until 10.00 a.m. Be outdoors and active between 10.00 a.m. and 4.00 p.m.; if there is no daylight between these hours, be near bright indoor light.

Drinks
No caffeine drinks today. Drink caffeine-free beverages. To help your digestive clock and avert constipation, continue drinking plenty of water (at least eight glasses a day), starting with a glass when you wake and a glass before each meal.

Meals
Eat lightly, with high-protein, low-fat breakfasts and lunches, and high-carbohydrate suppers. Suppers should include fruit (apples, pears, stewed prunes and figs), vegetables, wholegrain breads and high-fibre cereals, to keep your digestive system running smoothly. If constipation remains a problem, correct it gently with a soluble-fibre laxative.

Time Allowance
For best mental and physical activity and before the start of tours:
   —with the Beat Jet Lag Plan, allow two to three days
   —without the Beat Jet Lag Plan, allow seven to twelve days.
After your time allowance, schedule first appointments and activities in the late afternoon, after 4.00 p.m.

Plan 10 West

Watch set back 10 hours

Westbound flight

Flight examples:	Number of time zones:	Flying time: (hours)
Auckland to Athens	10	23.15
Delhi to New York	10½	18.45
London to Anchorage	9	9.00
London to Honolulu	10	18.45
Los Angeles to Bangkok	9	22.00
New York to Tokyo	10	13.45

This Plan is devised for westbound 9, 9½, 10 and 10½ time-zone changes. (The Plan could also be followed for a nonstop eastbound flight crossing fourteen time zones—although that is *not* a preferred itinerary.)

A nonstop flight of at least eight hours (some intercontinental flights take all day), and adding nine or more hours to the day on a westbound flight, is extremely fatiguing—especially for elderly travellers. You may want to break up the journey into sections with night stopovers, similar to a trip eastward. When coupled with your own determination, the Beat Jet Lag Plan will help you, every step of the way, to overcome the expected jet-lag symptoms and resynchronize your body to the new local time. Carefully follow the specified times for light exposure after landing.

Before flight
Sleep
The best idea is to pre-adjust your schedule before you leave, by a two, three or four hour phase-shift. Three days before you fly, get up and go to bed two hours later than usual. One day before you fly, make your day three hours later than usual.

Drinks
For three days before, stop drinking coffee, tea, cocoa, chocolate or cola drinks with caffeine, and avoid caffeine-containing drugs and diet aids. Switch to the caffeine-free beverages listed in Chapter 5. If you find it impossible to go without your usual uplifting cup, at least make it weak, and drink it only at about 4.00 p.m.

Meals
Three days before you fly, have mealtimes two hours later than usual. One day before you fly, have your meals three hours later than usual.

Start eating high-protein, low-fat breakfasts and lunches, and high-carbohydrate dinners, as outlined in Chapter 5. Eat small portions, so that your digestive system is not overloaded before you fly.

Flight day
(With a 10-hour time-shift, this day has 34 hours)

Best departure and arrival times
For a short flight, leave before 12.00 noon. For a long flight, choose one that arrives during your normal active phase, about 12.00 noon destination time.

Time change
Immediately you board the aircraft, set your watch back to the time at today's destination. Forget the old time zone, and focus on what you'll be doing after your flight.

Sleep
Because your day is going to be an extremely long one, try to sleep as late as possible. The early part of the flight will be the 'inactive' sleep phase at your destination, so try to rest and relax as much as you can, to reduce the fatigue of the expanded day and long flight.

Drinks
Take two strong cups of black coffee or tea in the morning *only*, between 7.00 a.m. and 11.00 a.m. (no cream or sugar, although sugar-free sweeteners are allowed). During the flight, drink plenty of water or fruit juices to counteract the aircraft's low humidity and dehydration. Avoid alcohol, or limit yourself to only one drink taken with a meal.

Meals
Eat lightly, trying to match mealtimes to those at your destination. Before catching the plane, eat a high-protein, low-fat breakfast and lunch. After boarding, a high-carbohydrate dinner will relax you for sleep during the flight. Towards the end of the flight, or after you land, have a light carbohydrate snack.

After flight
Sleep
After the westward flight, your body will naturally want to wake you early. Stay in bed as long as possible, with eyes closed, and continue complete

relaxation until normal local waking time. Stay active during the afternoon and early evening, and don't nap. If you are alone in the evening, turn on lively radio, television or video. Sleep according to local time.

Light

Be outdoors and active between 8.00 a.m. and 2.00 p.m. If there is no daylight outdoors between those hours, be near bright indoor light. Stay indoors between 2.00 p.m. and 6.00 p.m.

Drinks

No caffeine drinks today. To help your digestive clock and avert constipation, continue drinking plenty of water (at least eight glasses a day), starting with a glass when you wake and a glass before each meal.

Meals

Eat lightly until you feel fully adjusted, having high-protein, low-fat breakfasts and lunches, and high-carbohydrate dinners. Have carbohydrate evening snacks, if you like. Late snacks should include fruit (such as apples, pears, stewed prunes and figs), vegetables, wholegrain breads and high-fibre cereals, to keep your digestive system running smoothly. If constipation remains a problem, correct it gently with a soluble-fibre laxative.

Time Allowance

For best mental and physical activity, and before the start of tours:

   —with the Beat Jet Lag Plan, allow two days

   — without the Beat Jet Lag Plan, allow seven to ten days.

After your time allowance, schedule first appointments and activities in the mornings at an early hour.

Plan 12 East

Eastbound flight   Watch advanced 12 hours

Flight examples:	Number of time zones:	Flying time: (hours)
Chicago to Delhi	11½	18.15
London to Auckland	12	24.00
New York to Bangkok	12	22.00
New York to Jakarta	12	28.00
Papeete to Paris	11	20.00
Tokyo to Rio de Janeiro	12	23.30

This Plan is devised for eastbound 11, 11½, 12 and 12½ time-zone changes.

An eleven- or twelve-hour time advance gives your system the severest confusion. You may want to consider breaking the journey with stopovers at midway points for a night at an airport hotel, especially if your flight is halfway round the world and pole to pole. A twelve-hour time-shift is a complete reversal for your body clocks, forcing you to lose hours of sleep, to stay alert when you would rather be in bed, or giving you hours of night-time insomnia, and complete disorientation. With no countermeasures, your body could take weeks to reset its mechanisms to the 180-degree time-shift.

When there is no time to be lost, the Beat Jet Lag Plan specially created for this situation will help you to cut radically the time for adjustment and be in step with your far-flung destination. The times for light exposure after landing are especially important.

Before flight
Sleep
Try to set your body clocks in the right direction by pre-adjusting three or four hours in the few days before you commence your flight: rise and go to bed as early as you can manage. You can't fully adjust, of course, but you will have made a start in reaching the new time zone.

Drinks
For three days before the flight, stop drinking coffee, tea, chocolate, cocoa and cola drinks containing caffeine, and avoid caffeine-containing drugs and diet aids as listed in Chapter 5. Switch to the caffeine-free alternatives. If you can't go without your usual uplifting cup, at least make it weak and drink it only at about 4.00 p.m.

Meals

Eat your meals two or three hours earlier each day before the flight. Start eating high-protein, low-fat breakfasts and lunches, and high-carbohydrate suppers, as outlined in Chapter 5. On the day before the flight, eat lightly and skip any evening snack, so that your digestive system is not overburdened before you want it to adjust.

Flight day

(With a 12-hour time-shift, this day has only 12 hours)

Best departure and arrival times

A late departure before midnight, on a night flight is recommended, with arrival the next day after 6.00 a.m. destination time.

Time change

Immediately you board the aircraft, advance your watch to the time at today's destination. Forget the old time zone, and focus on what you'll be doing after your flight.

Sleep

On the morning of the flight, rise about two or three hours earlier than usual. During the flight, sleep if possible during what would be night time at your destination. When it is 11.00 p.m. at your destination, it would be 11.00 a.m. in the old zone; you won't feel tired, but close the cabin window-blinds, switch off the reading lights, arrange the pillow and blanket, close your eyes or wear an eye-mask if necessary, and relax for as long as possible.

Drinks

No caffeine-containing drinks or medicines in the morning or afternoon. Between 7.00 p.m. and 11.00 p.m. old time zone (wherever you may be) drink two cups of strong black coffee or tea (no cream or sugar, although sugar-free sweeteners are permitted). You may be flying for as long as twenty-four hours today, so drink plenty of water or fruit juices while in flight, to offset the aircraft dehydration. Avoid alcohol, or limit yourself to only one drink taken with a meal.

Meals

Eat small portions, with mealtimes according to today's destination.

Have a high-protein, low-fat breakfast. Having lunch is optional; if you do eat this meal, be sure it is high in protein and low in fat. Since this is a short day, you won't eat dinner or an evening snack.

After flight
Sleep
When day is night and night time is daytime, sleep and wake cycles are completely out of phase. Don't sleep late on arrival. Set your alarm clock or ask the hotel staff for a prompt wake-up call. Then rise and shine! Do the Energizing Exercises in Chapter 4 to rouse your body and brain. Resist the urge to nap during the day, and stay active. Retire to bed by 10.00 p.m. local time; you may feel wide awake, but make your room dark, get to bed, close your eyes and relax. Sleep will come. Chapter 7 gives ways to counteract insomnia and induce sleep.

Light
Be outdoors and active between 6.00 a.m. and 12.00 noon. If there is no daylight between these hours, be near bright indoor light. Remain indoors from 12.00 noon to 6.00 p.m.

Drinks
No caffeine drinks today. To help your digestive clock and avert constipation, continue drinking plenty of water (at least eight glasses a day), starting with a glass when you wake and a glass before each meal.

Meals
Eat small portions until you feel more adjusted, with mealtimes on local time. Have high-protein, low-fat breakfasts and lunches, and high-carbohydrate suppers. Suppers and late snacks should include fruit (such as apples, pears, stewed prunes and figs), vegetables, wholegrain breads and high-fibre cereals, to keep your digestive system running smoothly. If constipation remains a problem, correct it gently with a soluble-fibre laxative.

Time Allowance
For best mental and physical activity, and before the start of tours:
   —with the Beat Jet Lag Plan, allow three days;
   —without the Beat Jet Lag Plan, allow nine to twelve days.
After your time allowance, schedule first appointments and activities in the late afternoon or evening.

Plan 12 West

Watch set back 12 hours   Westbound flight

Flight examples:	Number of time zones:	Flying time: (hours)
Bombay to Chicago	11½	22.00
London to Nadi (via LA)	12	29.45
Moscow to Anchorage (via NY)	12	23.15
New York to Singapore	11	22.00
Singapore to Caracas	12	24.30
Washington to Bangkok	12	21.30

This Plan is devised for westbound 11, 11½, 12 and 12½ time-zone changes.

Zipping halfway round the world, across eleven or more time zones, west or east, is the most dramatic disturbance you can give your biological clocks, with the risk of total disorientation. As with an eastward flight, you should consider breaking the journey with intermediate stopovers at airport hotels to allow your circadian clocks to catch up and to let you have a good night's sleep.

Feel confident that the Plan has been specially devised for long-distance travellers to significantly reduce jet-lag symptoms; the effort you make to follow the Plan will determine the success in condensing the time of adjustment. With sleep/wake patterns completely reversed, the resetting of body clocks by means of specified hours of daylight or bright light is of prime importance in the Beat Jet Lag Plan. For details, follow Plan 12 East.

A GOOD NIGHT'S SLEEP

At any given hour of the day, as the world turns, an average of over 200 million people are getting up and another group are becoming sleepy—hoping for a good night's sleep. But after a long flight across several time zones has reversed night and day, a good night's sleep can be elusive.

Sleep is one of the most compelling mysteries in human life, and so powerful a force that none of us can go without it for long. Losing just a single night's sleep is enough to undermine decision making, and being even slightly deprived can seriously cramp your thinking the following day.

For sleep to begin, you need two things: your daytime-activity system must lessen, and your (weaker) sleep system must assert itself. Jet lag can create chaos in both systems. If you can't get off to sleep, either the neurotransmitters in your wake system are too active, or your sleep system isn't sufficiently strong.

How much sleep do you need?

Most adults sleep between seven and eight hours, some as little as three or four; a teenager may sleep for as long as nine or ten hours; an elderly person may nap during the day and then sleep only five hours a night. Five hours is about the least sleep that a person can tolerate; less than that can make you forgetful, jittery and irritable. With advancing age, some people change to shorter nights and some to longer ones. We all have varying needs: one person's idea of a good night might be what others call insomnia.

What causes insomnia?

Chronic insomnia usually stems from such conditions as heart disease, arthritis, diabetes, asthma, epilepsy or ulcers, or the medicines needed to help these conditions—or the long-term abuse of alcohol, drugs and sleeping pills.

Short-term insomnia, lasting up to three weeks, may happen when you are anxious, nervous, feeling physical and mental tension. Typical causes are the death of someone close, divorce, exams, worries about money, losing your job, or being excessively concerned about health.

Transient insomnia is the sleep disturbance caused by jet travel across several time zones, and, as the word implies, is only a temporary disorder lasting only a few days.

What is sleep?

Your body may look a picture of tranquillity while you sleep, but you don't simply 'fall' asleep. Numerous biochemical, physiological and psychological events are constantly taking place as you descend slowly through different levels.

As you close your eyes and drift off, you enter the first stage of what is called quiet sleep. Stage 1 is a sort of twilight zone between waking and sleeping. Your brain produces small rapid, irregular waves; muscles are relaxing; temperature is falling; breathing is becoming regular. In Stage 2 of quiet sleep, your brain waves become larger. You roll your eyes slowly. In Stage 3, your brain waves are slower and bigger. Bodily functions slow down even more. You are removed from the waking world. In Stage 4 (delta), you reach deepest sleep, the most profound state of unconsciousness, when you are 'dead to the world' and difficult to waken. These four stages of quiet sleep are often called non-REM or NREM sleep. Then, as you begin to move back up rapidly through the same sleep stages as before, you don't go all the way to full wakefulness but into active sleep, with irregular heart rate, blood-pressure and breathing—the stage referred to as Rapid Eye Movement or REM sleep. Slow rolling eye movements are typical for the entry into non-REM sleep; in contrast, during REM periods the pupils dart back and forth rapidly.

The entire cycle of non-REM and REM sleep takes about 90 minutes, so by the morning, you have gone round the sleep cycle four or five times, and been almost awake three or four times during a night of healthy sleep. Early in the night, the periods spent in the deepest stages of quiet sleep are longer. In the second half of the night, REM sleep predominates.

After a long jet flight, your first night of sleep has upsetting changes in rhythm: Rapid Eye Movement sleep when you usually experience deep dreaming beneficial for mental health is usually delayed or cut short; then on the following night you may get a 'REM rebound', when the period for REM sleep is increased and dreams are vivid.

What you can do for a good night's sleep

Following the Beat Jet Lag Plan, the high-carbohydrate foods eaten at suppertime or late snack should make you feel drowsy naturally. But if you have trouble dropping off during your night-time inactive phase, what can you do? What do you do when you are lying awake at three in the morning and wonder where in the world you are?

You *don't* want to turn on the light; you *don't* want to read a mind-stimulating book or watch an exciting late-night TV film; you *don't* want to order coffee and sandwiches from room service. What's the answer? Close your eyes. Relax. Be comfortable. Sleep *will* come. You can encourage a good night's sleep with several techniques. Here are twenty methods without using drugs.

1. A regular routine
After an eastbound flight, it's too easy to be a night owl, and then rise late in the morning; after going westbound, it's too easy to feel drowsy early evening, and then be up *before* the lark or dawn chorus. Resist these temptations. After a long jet flight across several time zones, go to bed at the *same* time every night—11.00 p.m. to 7.00 a.m. destination time, or whatever is usual for you. Set your alarm clock to wake you at the same time every morning. If you have a poor night's sleep, don't linger in bed or oversleep the next day. By establishing a regular routine, you help re-establish the biological rhythms in the new time zone, strengthening your circadian cycle, leading to a regular time for the onset of drowsiness and finally sleep.

2. No daytime naps
Daytime naps disrupt normal night-time sleep. Don't use them as a substitute for the poor sleep you had the previous night. Napping only prolongs jet lag. If you are a napper who sleeps poorly at night, your night-time sleep should improve if you skip the naps.

3. Exercise
Exercise in the daytime tends to benefit sleep at night. Following the Beat Jet Lag Plan, you start exercising as soon as you land, during the active phase of your day: walking, jogging, swimming or bicycling. Don't jump into a lot of exercise if you are usually sedentary; a walk during the day may be enough for you to be pleasantly tired later. But don't exercise right at bedtime. The best time is in late afternoon (so long as it ties in with your prescribed light-exposure period), to burn off the tensions that have accumulated during the day, and let the body and mind unwind.

4. Don't bring the office to bed
If you tend to lie in bed thinking of what you should have done during the day, or will need to do tomorrow, don't try to 'sleep on the problem'. Set

a planning- or worry-time to deal with these distractions *before* getting into bed. Make lists, write out problems and possible solutions—then *put them away.*

5. The right sleeping environment
Keep the light out of the bedroom. Light is one of your body's most powerful time cues, and early morning sun can stimulate your brain to full wakefulness long before you want it to. Close the curtains or draperies, or use a light-blocking shade, or wear an eye-mask. For many people, the ideal room temperature for sleep comfort is around 16 degrees C (61 degrees F). You'll stay under the covers longer in a cooler room, and be more restless in a stuffy overheated one. We all vary with our reactions to sound during the night. Women are much more likely than men to waken because of noise. Obviously, it's a good idea to book hotel rooms in quiet neighbourhoods. If outside noise is troubling and inescapable, turn on the room air-conditioner or electric fan for a steady hum to mask the noise. You could wear ear plugs—although they might make it harder to hear the wake-up alarm in the morning.

Once you are in bed, don't think about time. Turn the clock face to the wall. Then think sleep.

6. Should couples sleep together after a long trip?
Sleeping together may be good for marital bliss, but for the first night or two after a long flight when you are both feeling jet-lagged, separate beds can eliminate disturbed sleep if your partner is tossing. On the other hand, if you and your partner find sex mutually satisfying, having sex before sleep may release tensions, lift jet-lag depression, and create greater contentment so you both sleep well. Travelling with your helpmate can lighten jet-lag symptoms.

7. Develop a sleep ritual
At home or away, give yourself cues for your body to settle down for the night. Have a simple routine before you slide into bed: a few gentle stretches to release muscle tension, a warm bath with favourite bath-salts (a tablespoon of a balsam essence in your bath can be soothing), a few minutes of relaxing soft music or a few pages of poetry.

8. Bedtime snacks
Don't go to bed stuffed or starved. Unless you find that hunger keeps you awake, a snack is best avoided before bedtime if it is not specified

in the Beat Jet Lag Plan. A late snack can cause indigestion when your digestive system is out of phase. Antacids containing aluminium produce poor quality sleep.

9. Stay away from stimulants

Brain-wave patterns change during sleep in response to late-night **caffeine**, indicating a lower quality of sleep. Caffeine can make it harder for you to fall asleep, can reduce deep sleep, the total amount of sleep, and increase night-time wakenings. Other sleep-robbers: **prescription drugs** containing caffeine (including diet pills) and other stimulants (refer to Figure 4, the Caffeine Scorecard in Chapter 5); **tyrosine,** found in chocolate, Chianti wine and cheddar cheese; and **monosodium glutamate** (MSG), a seasoning often used in Chinese cooking. Other undesirable mind stimulants are watching exciting TV programmes or reading hair-raising fiction just before sleep.

10. Smoking

Nicotine is even stronger than caffeine as a stimulant of the nervous system, and can interfere with sleep. Heavy smokers take longer to fall asleep, wake more often and have less REM and deep non-REM sleep. Because nicotine withdrawal can start two to three hours after the last puff, some smokers can wake in the night craving a cigarette. Help yourself to better sleep by not smoking.

11. Alcohol

The effect of alcohol is deceiving. Too much alcohol with dinner can make it harder to *fall* asleep; too much at bedtime makes it harder to *stay* asleep. Moderate drinking may get you off to sleep, but the sleep will be fragmented, suppressing REM and deep non-REM sleep, and speeding the shifts between sleep stages. You will probably wake in the middle of the night when alcohol's relaxing effect wears off.

12. Sip a nightcap

No, not the alcoholic variety. If you can tolerate milk, a small glass is an old time-tested remedy (perhaps mixed with Horlicks, but not cocoa which contains caffeine). Milk has a small amount of natural l-tryptophan—an amino acid that is nature's sleeping pill—and may also provide other sleep-inducing chemicals.

13. Try to stay awake

It's a paradox, but it works. Rather than desperately worrying about falling asleep fast, try desperately to stay awake as long as you can. Stop wanting to sleep; tell yourself sleep doesn't really matter. With the pressure off, you can stop worrying—and start sleeping.

14. Relax your muscles
Learn progressive muscle relaxation, which involves alternate tensing and relaxing. Focus your attention on a specific group of muscles, such as those in your fists. Tense tightly for five seconds, then release for fifteen seconds. Repeat with other muscle groups.

15. Hypnotize yourself
As you lie in bed, breathe deeply, relax all your muscles, and repeat 'Sleep. I am sleepy. Sleep. I am sleepy' in time to the beat of your heart. You can buy a self-help recording with a mesmerizing message that you are becoming drowsy. Tapes are sold in book shops or can be ordered by post.

16. Sleepy-time tapes
In addition to 'white noise' tapes that provide a steady hum involving all frequencies, you can now buy environmental sounds—recordings of surf, rainfall or a waterfall—to lull you to sleep.

17. Visualization
Imagine you're lying on a beach—feeling the warm sun, smelling tropical blossoms, listening to the steady rhythm of waves lapping the shore—utterly relaxed. Or think black: imagine a black cat on a black velvet pillow on a black sofa on a black wool carpet in a black room.

18. Dreaming
Recall an interrupted dream, and try to get back into it to find out the finish.

19. A herbal pillow
Tuck into your suitcase a small pillow stuffed with a fragrant herbal blend, or a handful of kiln-dried hops tied in a muslin bag, to soothe you to sleep.

20. Yoga
Buy a book on *Savasana* yoga, to learn and master relaxation of every muscle, release tensions, and prepare for sleep.

Sleeping pills

The Beat Jet Lag Plan is a drug-free programme. The techniques you've just read are as effective as sleeping pills in the long run. They put *you* — and not a pill—in control. You may think of sleeping pills as wonder drugs that add hours of rest to the night, but at best they have only limited usefulness. Hundreds of studies have confirmed that sleeping pills increase sleep time by only about thirty minutes. They can be a temporary solution to insomnia, but they *don't* attempt to adjust your biological clocks and sleep/wake cycle. They should never be taken while you're on the plane.

All brands of prescribed sleeping pills are hypnotics—drugs that depress the central nervous system and put you to sleep. A variety of hypnotics are now on the market, including barbiturates, benzodiazepines and several classes of drugs generally referred to as nonbarbiturates/nonbenzodiazepines. Barbiturates suppress REM sleep; the benzodiazepines eliminate stages 3 and 4 of non-REM sleep. Refer to Typical Sleep-Inducing Medicines in Figure 5.

Active ingredient	Some trade names	Remarks
Benzodiazepines:		
Chlordiazepoxide	Librium	Constipation, dizziness,
Diazepam	Valium, Valcaps	drowsiness, headache,
Flurazepam	Dalmane	irritability, lethargy,
Lorazepam	Ativan	sweating, weakness. Can
Nitrazepam	Mogadon	interact with other drugs
Oxazepam	Serax, Serepax	and with alcohol. Ulcer
Temazepam	Restoril	medication may prolong
Triazolam	Halcion	side effects. Not for
		pregnant and nursing
		women. Can be habit-forming.
Barbiturates:		
Amobarbital	Amytal	Possible skin rash,
Butabarbital	Butisol	anaemia, depression,
Mephobarbital	Mebaral	dizziness, lethargy.
Pentobarbital	Nembutal	Possibly lethal with
Phenobarbital	Luminal	alcohol. Interferes with
Secobarbital	Seconal	anticoagulants,

Active ingredient	Some trade names	Remarks
		contraceptive pills, antiepilepsy drugs. Can create drug dependence. See also remarks for benzodiazepines.
Nonbarbiturate/nonbenzodiazepines:		
Chloral hydrate	Noctec	Dizziness, headache, lethargy, slurred speech, upset stomach. See also remarks for barbiturates.
Ethchlorvynol	Placidyl	
Ethinamate	Valmid	
Glutethimide	Doriden	
Methyprylon	Noludar	
Sedative antidepressant:		
Amitriptyline	Elavil, Endep, Tofranil, Vivactil	Constipation, dry mouth, weight gain.
Antihistamines:		
Diphenhydramine hydrochloride and diphenhydramine citrate	Compoz, Nervine, Nytol, Sleepinal, Sleepeze-3, Sominex, Sominex-2	Dizziness, double vision, dry mouth, nose and throat, nausea. Not for pregnant women, asthmatics, sufferers of glaucoma or enlarged prostate gland.
Doxylamine succinate	Doxysom, Unisom, Ultra Sleep	See above.

Figure 5: Typical Sleep-Inducing Medicines

They can be useful in certain situations. For instance, during the Falkland Islands War in 1982, the Royal Air Force showed that the careful strategic use of sleeping pills (mostly the short-acting *temazepam*) enhanced sleep and alertness in the round-the-clock operation, when crews were transporting 28,000 British troops and supplies a distance of 8,000 miles from bases five time zones away.

But in ordinary circumstances, these drugs eventually cause disturbed sleep, side-effects, a sleep 'hangover' the next day, and possible drug dependence. Because sleeping pills are widely available, you may have the mistaken impression that you can use them casually, but they should not be taken without your doctor's advice. If you use them frequently, your body tends to build up a tolerance, leading to increased use, more potent dosage and addiction. Once you stop taking the pills, 'rebound insomnia' brings sleep problems more severe than ever. Sleeping pills can be *fatal* when taken in combination with alcohol or with other drugs such as tranquillizers or sedatives. People who take sleeping pills should *never* drink for two days afterwards. Even when not fatal, combining drugs and alcohol can be dangerous when driving and using other machinery. Long-acting sleeping pills, by themselves, can impair driving skills the day after they are taken.

The older you are (especially if you are over 60), the more frequently toxic drug reactions can occur when using sleeping pills, or combining the pills with other drugs taken for medical problems. It takes your liver longer to break down these pills, so you feel the effects long after you get up the next morning. Never take sleeping pills if you have asthma, glaucoma, emphysema, chronic lung disease, shortness of breath, difficulty in breathing, sleep apnoea, a liver disorder or difficulty in urinating due to an enlarged prostate gland. Barbiturates decrease the effectiveness of drugs such as anticoagulants. Sleeping pills can cause older people to stumble or fall, feel groggy, hung-over or confused. They make you forgetful, slow down reaction times and interfere with being able to think clearly and quickly.

Pregnant and nursing women should be aware that sleeping pills may harm their foetus or child. If you are pregnant, or want to become pregnant, ask your doctor whether it is safe or advisable to use any drug. Never give sleeping pills to children under twelve.

Sleeping pills should only be taken under a doctor's supervision—whether prescription or non-prescription—and only the smallest effective dose for the shortest possible time. Never accept anyone else's prescription or non-prescription sleeping aid.

Doctors today are not so quick to reach for the prescription pad and tend not to prescribe barbiturates. Prescriptions now are usually for one of the benzodiazepines or similar drug, considered less addictive and safer than barbiturates. The benzodiazepines are still *very* toxic, however, when taken in combination with alcohol, or when overdoses are taken if you have a respiratory disorder. Not all benzodiazepines are alike, though: some work faster than others, some produce effects that last longer, and some are eliminated sooner.

The sleeping pill of the 1970s was *flurazepam* (Dalmane), considered safer than barbiturates, but it remains active in the central nervous system for at least 80 hours, giving you daytime drowsiness afterwards.

Most benzodiazepines have active by-products that remain in your body longer than most barbiturates. *Triazolam* (Halcion), a benzodiazepine, dissipates relatively quickly, but has been linked to several cases of temporary memory loss, malaise, ennui, and next-day grogginess.

Non-prescription sleeping pills also can produce disturbing side-effects, including disorientation, dizziness, ringing in the ears, poor coordination, blurred or double vision and irritability.

Although the health supplement L-Tryptophan *had* been used in the past as a mild non-prescription aid to sleep, either on its own or combined with other ingredients as a 'special formula' for jet lag, products with this substance have now been banned for sale. Until current problems with L-Tryptophan have been resolved, readers are warned not to take this supplement because of the link with the sometimes-fatal blood and muscle ailment called eosinophilia-myalgia syndrome (EMS). Other illnesses traced to L-Tryptophan have been fever, weakness, severe muscle and joint pain, shortness of breath, swelling of legs and feet, and pneumonia.

As a postscript to this chapter on sleep, teams of researchers are testing a melatonin pill which seems to reset the body's internal biological clock. Melatonin, the naturally-produced hormone of the pineal, has now been synthesized from a byproduct of a coffee decaffeination method. At the time of writing, the product awaits government approval, and the correct formula and dosage are still being worked out. Because it is a hormone with a similar structure to oestrogen, the question of dosage is critical as the risk of side-effects such as cancer is serious. An overdose of melatonin could also produce too much sleepiness and affect productivity the following day. However, synthetic melatonin seems to hold great promise in the future as the pill to treat transient insomnia caused by jet lag.

FLIGHT TIPS FROM FREQUENT FLYERS

Altitude sickness

If the aircraft is not properly pressurized, over 8000 feet you may suffer altitude sickness, to add to your jet-lag problems. Many people have shortness of breath, some get headaches, lose appetite, feel nauseous and light-headed. It should go away naturally in twenty-four to thirty-six hours. At high altitudes, dehydration occurs at a faster rate, producing dizziness and confusion. If you have other medical problems, dehydration can make them worse. An important rule is to drink plenty of water during any flight.

Blind travellers

Circadian cycles depend on intact eyes and normal nerve transmission; although blind people have biological rhythms, they can differ from those of the sighted by having less pronounced peaks and lows. To beat jet lag, the blind need to concentrate on cues other than light exposure, using the sounds and noises around them, talking with people, taking exercise, and following the meal plans in Chapter 5.

Blind people should book their flights as far ahead as possible and tell the airline of the disability. For safety reasons, the airlines may limit the number of disabled passengers they will accept for any particular flight. The blind don't need to be accompanied by anyone else; airline personnel are willing to help if they are given advance notice. A 'Seeing Eye' dog is accepted by some airlines in the cabin, providing quarantine regulations allow the animal into the country being visited. (The United Kingdom does *not* permit the entry of such dogs, due to strict enforcement of quarantine laws.)

Clothing

Make sure you dress comfortably, so that you travel relaxed and sleep relaxed. You may be reaching your destination in time for bed, or need to be prepared for sleep on the plane.

On long flights, veteran travellers wear soft, loose-fitting clothes of easy-care fabrics that are stain- and crease-resistant. Keep handy a lightweight wool sweater or cardigan (easier than a jacket), in case air-conditioning turns cold. You'll need it when you become sleepy, and when body temperature drops during your inactive night phase. Avoid tight underwear and stockings that interfere with circulation. On the other hand, if you have varicose veins or circulation problems, consider wearing elastic support hose. Wear worn shoes that you *know* are comfortable; remove them during flight and put them back on an hour before landing. Shoes with laces are easier if your feet swell. Tuck a pair of soft slippers into your flight bag, together with a shoe horn (they are standard features provided free in first- and business-class).

Contact lenses and glasses

Remove them during a long flight and store them carefully. The dehydrating cabin atmosphere and re-circulating cigarette smoke can irritate your eyes and make wearing lenses uncomfortable. Carry a spare set of contacts, glasses or their prescriptions, in case you lose or break them during the trip.

Dental work

Have a pre-trip dental examination to avoid problems in-flight and emergency treatment when you are abroad. A badly-filled tooth will almost certainly give you toothache when the plane reaches high altitude. As the plane climbs, the air trapped behind the filling expands, causing pain. If this happens, see a dentist immediately you land.

Disabled travellers

Be sure to book your seat far in advance as seating may be limited. Many airlines have restrictions on the number of disabled passengers they will accept for any particular flight. Tell the airline of your disability. Government safety regulations won't allow you to use your own wheelchair during the flight, but ask the airline if you can take it aboard the plane or should check it as luggage.

Using the toilets can present special problems for handicapped people. Some book a seat next to the lavatory. Others try to minimize trips to the toilet by cutting down on liquid consumption before and during flight, but there is a dangerous risk of becoming dehydrated—only do so on your doctor's advice. Your doctor may suggest medicines that can help.

Diving

If you're a scuba enthusiast, *don't* dive within forty-eight hours of a flight. You can get the bends even in a pressurized aircraft if you have been scuba-diving a short time before flying. Bends are caused by the release of nitrogen bubbles from your blood—bubbles that collect around joints and in muscles, press against nerves, and cause pain. Bends, and other complications from flying too soon after diving, are dangerous.

Drugs and medicines

Because long flights cause unusual and sometimes weird reactions to medicine, take only essential medication. Ask your doctor in advance about daily dosage when flights take you through eight or more time zones: should you decrease the dose when you fly east? Will you need an extra half-dose at your westward destination? Get a letter from your doctor if you must carry syringes and needles, to avert problems with Customs authorities.

Ear plugs

Plugs can block out aircraft noise when you are trying to sleep during the flight. They can be waxy, foam-rubber or rubber. The wax and foam-rubber types are moulded or squeezed between the fingers to fit inside your ear canal, and are disposable. Rubber plugs are premoulded, washable and supposed to be reusable, but it is better to discard them after use to avoid infecting your ears. Whichever style of plugs you choose, be sure they are clean before inserting them. Plugs are usually sold in chemists, drug stores, sporting-goods shops and airport shops.

If you forget to buy a set of ear plugs, wear the airline-supplied headset (with the volume turned down) to block out disturbing aircraft noise.

Ear-popping and ear pain

Many jet-setters become aware of ear problems linked to high-altitude travel. The pressure changes that occur during the flight, especially when you are about to land, can cause acute ear discomfort. This happens when the pressure-regulating eustachian tube between your middle ear and the air chamber behind the nose (nasopharynx) becomes blocked. Several manoeuvres can help:

- Avoid sleeping when the plane is about to land.
- Swallow frequently.
- Eat a sweet or chew gum.
- Pinch nostrils, take a deep breath, then gently blow your nose against your fingers.
- Use a mild decongestant (inhaler, spray, drops or tablets) an hour or

so before landing. (If you have heart disease, high blood-pressure, irregular heart rhythms, thyroid disease or excessive nervousness, you should probably avoid decongestants.)

● If you are travelling with a baby, give a bottle or dummy (pacifier) for sucking.

If you have a cold while travelling, you are more likely to develop ear pain. Use a decongestant before you board the aircraft and again when the pilot announces the descent for landing.

Expectant mothers
Ask your doctor if you may fly or need to take precautions during flight. Frequent travel at high altitude during pregnancy may expose the developing foetus to increased amounts of radiation.

Pregnancy can intensify motion sickness and flying can bring on an attack of morning sickness. When booking the flight, inform the airline of your special condition. Wear your seat-belt low, to minimize pressure on your abdomen.

Eye-drops
Eyes often feel dry and inflamed during a long flight. Be prepared: pack a bottle of eye-drops in your flight bag, ready to soothe and moisten your eyes and remove redness. Read the instructions on the label. Don't let the dropper touch your eyelashes or eyes; don't place the dropper on the lavatory counter. If you think you might have trouble using eye-drops, get someone to help you.

Eye-masks
These are standard features in first- and business-class. Use the one provided or bring your own, to shut out cabin lights when you need to sleep during your inactive phase. Some masks have nose-clips to keep them in place; others have bands of elastic; some are washable, which can be a handy feature if you wear them over make-up or skin cream. You can usually buy masks at airport shops.

Lack of oxygen (hypoxia)
If you know you have a cardiac or lung problem, ask your doctor before the flight about necessary precautions. Low oxygen supply at high altitudes can be critical for people with emphysema or heart disease, and can cause unconsciousness and even death.

Before take-off, become familiar with the plane's emergency oxygen system and ask the flight attendant how to use it in flight. Atmospheric pressure decreases at higher altitudes; consequently aircraft are designed to provide artificial pressure for sufficient oxygen to reach your lungs; supplementary oxygen is rarely needed in pressurized aircraft. Too little oxygen (hypoxia) acts much like alcohol in exhilarating you and giving a false self-confidence; euphoria is usually the first obvious symptom of hypoxia. Headache, blurred vision, drowsiness and impaired coordination are later symptoms which should urge you to ask the flight attendant for an oxygen mask. Danger comes in not immediately recognizing the need for it.

Motion sickness

A queasy stomach during flight can increase jet-lag problems when you land. Even if you usually suffer car- or sea-sickness, you shouldn't feel symptoms in a modern jet since large aircraft are now designed to be stable—but of course they are still subject to rough-weather turbulence which could be your undoing. Here's your strategy:

- When booking your flight, choose a seat midships, between the wings, away from the food odours of the flight attendants' galleys and the staleness of the lavatories.

- Don't eat rich high-fat foods or anything fried.

- Don't drink alcohol.

- When you feel queasy, don't look out at the horizon and don't read. Drink plenty of water. Loosen your clothes around throat and waist. Point the air-conditioning directly at your face, tilt your seat back as far as possible and close your eyes. A cool scented towel from the flight attendant can be refreshing on face, neck and hands.

- If you are a chronic victim of motion sickness, consult your doctor for a prescription or before taking non-prescription remedies (to be sure they are compatible with any other medicine you take). Most anti-nausea medicines are antihistamines (cyclizine, meclizine, dimenhydrinate) which can make you sleepy and affect your coordination—a dangerous condition if you intend to drive as soon as you land.

- A new non-drug aid to ward off motion sickness is worn on the wrist. It presses on the anti-nausea acupressure point and can be worn continuously and used repeatedly. You can buy them at leading chemists or drug stores.

Nutritional supplements

As 'flight insurance' before extensive travel, it makes good sense to have a healthy balanced diet including foods with vitamins A, C, E and beta carotene. For frequent travellers who are concerned with the fatigue and stress in the body which may occur as a result of high-altitude flying, special supplements are available. These supplements are a combination of 'supersprouts' derived from wheat, and contain enzymes that deal with possible oxidative stresses during jet travel: 'Jet Stress' can be ordered by post from Biomed Foods, 1215 Center Street, Honolulu, HI 96816-3226 (telephone for information: 1-800-331-5888). A similar enzyme product called 'JetZyme' may be obtained from Viator Ltd., P.O. Box 747, Guildford, Surrey GU1 3QW, England (telephone for information: 0483-33481).

Pillows

Tuck an inflatable contour-pillow into your flight bag. Shaped to fit around your neck, it will gently support and cradle your head, helping you to sleep during the flight without neck soreness. You can buy these pillows at chemists, drug stores, luggage departments and airport gift shops.

Seating choice

To combat jet lag, you want to relax on board as much as possible. Ask your travel agent for a seat allocation at the time of booking, or get to the airport terminal in plenty of time to make a good seat choice, away from busy and noisy areas in the cabin. Choice seats are on the aisle and as far forward as possible. This position has less engine noise and lets you walk around occasionally to stretch your legs. If you are extra tall, a seat in the rows near the doors often has more leg-room. Unless you are physically handicapped, avoid sitting near the lavatories; sleeping will be difficult if crowds are queueing to use them, and meals may seem unappetizing in an atmosphere of stale toilets.

If you are travelling with an infant, choose a seat facing a bulkhead where many airlines provide carry-cots (bassinets). If you don't have a child with you, avoid these rows of seats designed for young families; noises could be disturbing when you try to sleep or nap.

If airline regulations allow smoking, the smoking section is usually in the rear because air-conditioning jets blow from front to back. If you must have a cigarette, choose a seat in the first row of the smoking section; you will have no one else's smoke drifting back and bothering you. See also **Smoking**.

Sinuses

Your sinuses, which are lined with mucous membranes, have openings to the outside; changes in pressure at high altitude can cause interior gases to expand and contract, producing sinus pain. Sinus membranes irritated from an allergy can swell and secrete a thick mucus, and that also causes pain. Nasal drops or sprays relieve the problems, but serious allergies may need oral medicines to open the cavities.

Sitting positions

Prolonged sitting is fatiguing and causes aches and pains in muscles and joints, but proper sitting helps prevent these aches and pains, sore backs and swollen feet. Keep your seat upright, put a pillow in the small of your back and fasten the seat belt snugly around your hips. Keep the back of your thighs off the seat by slightly raising your feet. Rest your feet on your briefcase, bag or blanket, to reduce vibrations from the aircraft. Don't cross your legs; don't keep your legs tightly pressed against the seat or up against the seat in front of you—both positions interfere with blood circulation. Crossing your legs also shifts body weight to your lower back and can bring on back pain. If the seat-belt sign is off and the pilot has announced it's OK to move around, spend a few minutes every hour walking in place and up the aisle. Wiggle your toes and lift your feet occasionally to get blood flowing back to your heart. Do the Energizing Exercises in Chapter 4.

Skin care

Low humidity in the aircraft cabin can dry your skin. Throughout the trip, slather on skin moisturizer, hand cream and lip-balm; drink plenty of water.

Smoking

Reduce your smoking, two days before flying and stop smoking several hours before the flight. Don't smoke on the plane. In any case, *all* smoking is banned on flights within the United States, Canada, and on certain European airlines. This is a good time to quit—for good. Smoking (yours and everybody else's) irritates the eyes, nose and throat linings; smoke can actually make you temporarily anaemic by reducing the haemoglobin in your blood; low cabin humidity and reduced oxygen in the cabin's air can increase the amount of carbon monoxide absorbed into the bloodstream, reducing the oxygen carried by your blood. Less oxygen makes your heart work harder, resulting in fatigue—and being fatigued makes your body clocks more confused. Smoking reacts with medicines, and may increase chances of blood clots forming in your legs, especially when you're forced to sit for several hours.

Passive smoke, the kind you inhale from other people's cigarettes, can be a real hazard. Choose a seat five or more rows in front of the smoking section, so that the air-conditioning will keep other people's smoke away from you.

Swollen feet and ankles

Many air travellers suffer puffy ankles and feet during long flights. If your airline seat has a flip-up footrest, use it to raise your legs and lift your feet off the deck. If a footrest is not provided, improvise with your briefcase, flight bag or a folded blanket. When you arrive at your destination, and it is your daytime active phase, ask room service for two large ice-buckets of ice. Soak each foot for a few minutes, to reduce swelling.

Vaccinations

If you need certain vaccinations and inoculations for visiting some areas around the world, complete the full set of shots well in advance of your flight in case you suffer any reactions or side-effects.

Wristwatches

To make sure your timing is perfect anywhere around the globe, several leading watchmakers now have styles that include two watches in one: two movements, one each for 'home' and 'away' time when travelling or making international phone calls. Another style features 'universal time', showing the time in other cities and time zones around the world.

Have a good flight! Happy landing!

FLYING FROM LONDON [1]

To:	Time Zones (hours from GMT)	Flight Time (hours)	Distance	
			(km)	(miles)
Accra, Ghana	GMT	7.00	5,120	3,180
Anchorage, Alaska[2]	−9	9.00	7,190	4,470
Athens[2]	+2	3.45	2,400	1,490
Auckland[3] (via Los Angeles)	−12	24.00	19,260	11,970
Bahrain	+3	6.30	5,070	3,150
Bangkok	+7	12.00	9,530	5,920
Beijing[2]	+8	17.15	8,130	5,050
Berlin[2]	+1	1.45	930	580
Bermuda[2]	−4	7.15	5,540	3,440
Bombay	+5½	9.00	7,190	4,470
Brussels[2]	+1	1.00	340	210
Buenos Aires[3] (via Madrid)	−3	16.15	11,330	7,040
Cairo[2]	+2	4.45	3,520	2,190
Cape Town	+2	13.00	9,690	6,020
Caracas	−4	9.30	7,550	4,690
Chicago[2]	−6	8.30	6,360	3,950
Colombo, Sri Lanka	+5½	12.15	8,710	5,410
Dar es Salaam	+3	10.45	7,500	4,660
Denver[2]	−7	9.45	7,530	4,680
Frankfurt[2]	+1	1.30	680	420
Helsinki[2]	+2	2.45	1,830	1,140
Hong Kong	+8	13.00	9,640	5,990
Honolulu (via Los Angeles)	−10	18.45	12,870	8,000
Istanbul[2]	+2	3.45	2,510	1,560
Johannesburg	+2	11.30	9,240	5,740
Larnaca, Cyprus[2]	+2	4.30	3,250	2,020
Lima, Peru (via Miami)	−5	17.00	10,300	6,400

To:	Time Zones (hours from GMT)	Flight Time (hours)	Distance (km)	(miles)
Los Angeles[2]	−8	11.00	8,770	5,450
Madrid[2]	+1	2.15	1,260	780
Manila	+8	18.15	12,830	7,970
Melbourne[3] (via Singapore)	+10	24.00	17,830	11,080
Mexico City (via Miami)	−6	14.00	8,920	5,540
Moscow[2]	+3	3.45	2,490	1,550
Muscat, Oman	+4	7.30	6,150	3,820
Nadi, Fiji (via Los Angeles)	−12	29.45	17,990	11,180
Nairobi	+3	8.30	6,840	4,250
New York[2]	−5	7.30	5,570	3,460
Oslo[2]	+1	2.00	1,170	730
Pago Pago (via Los Angeles)	−11	28.45	17,910	11,130
Panama City (via Miami)	−5	14.30	8,800	5,470
Papeete (via Los Angeles)	−10	21.30	15,390	9,560
Paris[2]	+1	1.15	350	220
Perth, W. Australia	+8	21.30	14,500	9,010
Reykjavik	GMT	3.00	1,900	1,180
Rio de Janeiro	−3	11.30	9,270	5,760
Riyadh	+3	6.00	5,120	3,180
Rome[2]	+1	2.30	1,450	900
Santiago, Chile[3] (via Rio)	−4	20.00	12,150	7,550
Singapore	+8	13.15	11,780	7,320
Stockholm[2]	+1	2.30	1,450	900
Sydney[3] (via Singapore)	+10	22.00	18,070	11,230
Tehran	+3½	5.45	4,860	3,020
Tel Aviv[2]	+2	4.30	3,720	2,310
Tokyo	+9	11.45	9,590	5,960
Toronto[2]	−5	8.00	5,730	3,560
Valletta, Malta[2]	+1	3.15	2,090	1,300
Vancouver, B.C.[2]	−8	9.30	7,600	4,720

To:	Time Zones (hours from GMT)	Flight Time (hours)	Distance (km)	(miles)
Vienna[2]	+1	2.15	1,260	780
Warsaw[2]	+1	2.30	1,450	900
Washington, D.C.[2]	−5	8.15	5,920	3,680

1. Time zones are regardless of the International Date Line and Daylight Saving Time; + hours are east of Greenwich Mean Time, with clocks advanced; − hours are west of Greenwich Mean Time, with clocks turned back. Flight Time is approximate, including connection. Distance is via normal airline route and noted connection.

2. Cities that may have Daylight Saving Time (usually one hour) approximately between April and October.

3. Cities that may have Daylight Saving Time (usually one hour) approximately between October and April.

(Source: Adapted from the *ABC World Airways Guide* and the *Official Airline Guide*.)

FLYING FROM NEW YORK [1]

To:	Time Zones (hours from EST)	Flight Time (hours)	Distance (km)	(miles)
Anchorage[2] (via Chicago)	−4	10.00	5,760	3,580
Athens[2]	+7	9.00	7,930	4,930
Auckland[3] (via Los Angeles)	−7	19.45	14,480	9,000
Bahrain	+8	14.45	10,630	6,610
Bangkok (via Tokyo)	−12	21.00	15,460	9,610
Beijing[2] (via Tokyo)	−11	24.15	12,420	7,720
Berlin[2]	+6	9.45	6,390	3,970
Bermuda[2]	+1	2.15	1,220	760
Bombay (via London)	+10½	17.30	12,610	7,840
Brussels[2]	+6	7.15	5,410	3,660
Buenos Aires[3]	+2	10.15	8,530	5,300
Cairo[2]	+7	8.30	9,030	5,610
Calgary[2]	−2	7.45	3,280	2,040
Cape Town (via London)	+7	20.00	15,250	9,480
Caracas	+1	4.30	3,410	2,120
Casablanca	+5	6.45	5,810	3,610
Chicago[2]	−1	2.30	1,170	730
Colombo (via Frankfurt)	+10½	23.15	14,270	8,870
Dallas[2]	−1	3.45	2,250	1,400
Denver[2]	−2	4.15	2,610	1,620
Frankfurt[2]	+6	7.00	6,190	3,850
Helsinki[2]	+7	8.00	6,610	4,110
Hong Kong	−11	20.30	13,150	8,170
Honolulu	−5	13.30	8,000	4,970
Istanbul[2]	+7	12.00	8,060	5,010

To:	Time Zones (hours from EST)	Flight Time (hours)	Distance (km)	(miles)
Johannesburg (via London)	+7	16.30	12,840	7,980
Larnaca, Cyprus[2] (via London)	+7	11.45	8,820	5,480
Lima, Peru	EST	9.30	5,870	3,650
London[2]	+5	6.45	5,570	3,460
Los Angeles[2]	−3	6.00	3,990	2,480
Madrid[2]	+6	7.00	5,780	3,590
Manila (via San Francisco)	−11	23.30	13,870	8,620
Melbourne[3] (via Los Angeles)	−9	24.00	16,750	10,410
Mexico City (via Atlanta)	−1	7.30	3,380	2,100
Moscow[2]	+8	9.00	7,510	4,670
Muscat, Oman (via London)	+9	17.00	11,710	7,280
Nadi, Fiji (via Los Angeles)	−7	21.30	13,210	8,210
Nairobi (via London)	+8	13.30	12,410	7,710
Oslo[2]	+6	7.30	5,920	3,680
Pago Pago (via Honolulu)	−6	22.15	12,200	7,580
Panama City	EST	4.45	3,560	2,210
Papeete (via Los Angeles)	−5	15.30	10,570	6,570
Paris[2]	+6	7.00	5,840	3,630
Perth, W. Australia (via Los Angeles)	−11	28.30	19,290	11,990
Reykjavik	+5	5.45	4,180	2,600
Rio de Janeiro	+2	9.00	7,850	4,880
Riyadh	+8	12.00	10,560	6,560
Rome[2]	+6	8.00	6,890	4,280
San Juan, Puerto Rico	+1	4.30	2,570	1,600
Santiago, Chile[3]	+1	12.30	8,250	5,130
Seattle[2]	−3	6.00	3,890	2,420

To:	Time Zones (hours from EST)	Flight Time (hours)	Distance (km)	(miles)
Seoul	−10	17.00	12,050	7,490
Shannon[2]	+5	6.15	4,960	3,080
Singapore (via Tokyo)	−11	26.00	16,170	10,050
Stockholm[2]	+6	7.30	6,310	3,920
Sydney[3] (via Los Angeles)	−9	21.15	16,030	9,960
Tel Aviv[2]	+7	10.15	9,160	5,690
Tokyo	−10	13.45	10,840	6,740
Valletta, Malta[2] (via London)	+6	11.30	7,660	4,760
Vienna[2]	+6	8.30	6,810	4,230

1. Time zones are regardless of the International Date Line and Daylight Saving Time; + hours are east of Eastern Standard Time, with clocks advanced; − hours are west of Eastern Standard Time, with clocks turned back. Flight Time is approximate, including connection. Distance is via normal airline route and noted connection.

2. Cities that may have Daylight Saving Time (usually one hour) approximately between April and October.

3. Cities that may have Daylight Saving Time (usually one hour) approximately between October and April.

(Source: Adapted from the *ABC World Airways Guide* and the *Official Airline Guide*.)

FLYING FROM SYDNEY[1]

To:	Time Zones (hours from SYD)	Flight Time (hours)	Distance (km)	(miles)
Amsterdam[2]	−9	26.00	16,880	10,490
Athens[2]	−8	20.00	15,350	9,540
Auckland[3]	+2	3.00	2,160	1,340
Bahrain (via Singapore)	−7	16.45	12,550	7,800
Bali	−3	7.15	4,620	2,870
Bangkok	−3	9.30	7,550	4,690
Beijing[2]	−2	13.00	9,160	5,690
Belgrade[2]	−9	25.15	15,710	9,760
Bombay	−4½	14.15	10,220	6,350
Brussels[2] (via London)	−9	25.45	18,410	11,440
Buenos Aires[3]	+11	16.00	12,490	7,760
Cairo[2] (via Singapore)	−8	19.30	14,560	9,050
Chicago[2]	+8	19.00	14,870	9,240
Christchurch, N.Z.[3]	+2	3.00	2,120	1,320
Colombo, Sri Lanka	−4½	12.45	9,040	5,620
Darwin, N.T.	−½	5.30	3,150	1,960
Delhi	−4½	14.30	10,450	6,490
Frankfurt[2] (via Bahrain)	−9	24.45	16,990	10,560
Harare	−8	16.30	11,270	7,000
Helsinki[2] (via London)	−8	22.00	15,430	9,590
Hong Kong	−2	9.00	7,390	4,590
Honolulu	+4	9.15	8,180	5,080
Istanbul[2] (via Singapore)	−8	22.30	14,970	9,300
Johannesburg (via Harare)	−8	20.30	12,230	7,600

To:	Time Zones (hours from SYD)	Flight Time (hours)	Distance (km)	(miles)
Kuala Lumpur	−2	8.15	6,630	4,120
Lima, Peru (via Los Angeles)	+9	24.30	18,800	11,680
London[2] (via Singapore)	−10	25.00	18,070	11,230
Los Angeles[2]	+6	13.30	12,070	7,500
Madrid[2] (via Bangkok)	−9	26.00	17,730	11,020
Manila	−2	7.45	6,260	3,890
Mauritius (via Singapore)	−6	16.30	9,170	5,700
Mexico City (via Los Angeles)	+8	20.00	14,560	9,050
Miami[2] (via Los Angeles)	+9	22.00	15,820	9,830
Moscow[2] (via London)	−7	30.15	20,570	12,780
Nadi, Fiji	+2	3.45	3,170	1,970
Nairobi (via Bombay)	−7	24.00	14,760	9,170
New York[2] (via Los Angeles)	+9	21.00	16,030	9,960
Norfolk Island	+1½	2.30	1,670	1,040
Noumea, New Caledonia	+1	2.45	1,980	1,230
Pago Pago	+3	5.15	4,410	2,740
Papeete	+4	9.00	6,260	3,890
Paris[2] (via Singapore)	−9	24.15	17,770	11,040
Perth, W.A.	−2	4.30	3,280	2,040
Port Moresby, P.N.G.	0	3.45	2,750	1,710
Rarotonga[3] (via Auckland)	+4	7.45	5,180	3,220
Rio de Janeiro (via B. Aires)	+11	21.30	14,470	8,990
Rome[2] (via Singapore)	−9	23.45	16,370	10,170

To:	Time Zones (hours from SYD)	Flight Time (hours)	Distance (km)	(miles)
San Francisco[2]	+6	15.30	12,040	7,480
Santiago, Chile[3] (via B. Aires)	+10	21.00	13,630	8,470
Seoul (via Tokyo)	−1	15.30	10,480	6,510
Singapore	−2	7.45	6,310	3,920
Stockholm[2] (via (London)	−9	27.45	19,510	12,120
Taipei (via Hong Kong)	−2	11.30	8,180	5,080
Tokyo	−1	9.30	9,290	5,770
Toronto[2]	+9	19.15	15,560	9,670
Vancouver, B.C.[2]	+6	16.00	12,520	7,780
Vienna[2]	−9	22.00	16,010	9,950
Warsaw[2] (via Vienna)	−9	24.15	16,530	10,270
Washington, D.C.[2] (via Los Angeles)	+9	21.00	15,760	9,790
Wellington, N.Z.[3]	+2	3.00	2,240	1,390

1. Time zones are regardless of the International Date Line and Daylight Saving Time; + hours are east of Sydney Standard Time, with clocks advanced; − hours are west of Sydney Standard Time, with clocks turned back. Flight Time is approximate, including connection. Distance is via normal airline route and noted connection.

2. Cities that may have Daylight Saving Time (usually one hour) approximately between April and October.

3. Cities that may have Daylight Saving Time (usually one hour) approximately between October and April.

(Source: Adapted from the *ABC World Airways Guide* and the *Official Airline Guide*.)

TIME ZONES BETWEEN MAJOR CITIES

From: \ To:	Athens	Auckland	Bangkok	Beijing	Bermuda	Bombay	Cairo	Chicago	Hong Kong	Honolulu	Johannesburg
Athens	—	10	5	6	6	3½	0	8	6	12	0
Auckland	10	—	5	4	8	6½	10	6	4	2	10
Bangkok	5	5	—	1	11	1½	5	11	1	7	5
Beijing	6	4	1	—	12	2½	6	10	0	6	6
Bermuda	6	8	11	12	—	9½	6	2	12	6	6
Bombay	3½	6½	1½	2½	9½	—	3½	11½	2½	8½	3½
Cairo	0	10	5	6	6	3½	—	8	6	12	0
Chicago	8	6	11	10	2	11½	8	—	10	4	8
Hong Kong	6	4	1	0	12	2½	6	10	—	6	6
Honolulu	12	2	7	6	6	8½	12	4	6	—	12
Johannesburg	0	10	5	6	6	3½	0	8	6	12	—
Lima	7	7	12	11	1	10½	7	1	11	5	7
Los Angeles	10	4	9	8	4	10½	10	2	8	2	10
Madrid	1	11	6	7	5	4½	1	7	7	11	1
Mexico City	8	6	11	10	2	11½	8	0	10	4	8
Moscow	1	9	4	5	7	2½	1	9	5	11	1
Nairobi	1	9	4	5	7	2½	1	9	5	11	1
New York	7	7	12	11	1	10½	7	1	11	5	7
Paris	1	11	6	7	5	4½	1	7	7	11	1
R. de Janeiro	5	9	10	11	1	8½	5	3	11	7	5
Riyadh	1	9	4	5	7	2½	1	9	5	11	1
Rome	1	11	6	7	5	4½	1	7	7	11	1
Singapore	6	4	1	0	12	2½	6	10	0	6	6
Sydney	8	2	3	2	10	4½	8	8	2	4	8
Tokyo	7	3	2	1	11	3½	7	9	1	5	7

Lima	Los Angeles	Madrid	Mexico City	Moscow	Nairobi	New York	Paris	R. de Janeiro	Riyadh	Rome	Singapore	Sydney	Tokyo
7	10	1	8	1	1	7	1	5	1	1	6	8	7
7	4	11	6	9	9	7	11	9	9	11	4	2	3
12	9	6	11	4	4	12	6	10	4	6	1	3	2
11	8	7	10	5	5	11	7	11	5	7	0	2	1
1	4	5	2	7	7	1	5	1	7	5	12	10	11
10½	10½	4½	11½	2½	2½	10½	4½	8½	2½	4½	2½	4½	3½
7	10	1	8	1	1	7	1	5	1	1	6	8	7
1	2	7	0	9	9	1	7	3	9	7	10	8	9
11	8	7	10	5	5	11	7	11	5	7	0	2	1
5	2	11	4	11	11	5	11	7	11	11	6	4	5
7	10	1	8	1	1	7	1	5	1	1	6	8	7
—	3	6	1	8	8	0	6	2	8	6	11	9	10
3	—	9	2	11	11	3	9	5	11	9	8	6	7
6	9	—	7	2	2	6	0	4	2	0	7	9	8
1	2	7	—	9	9	1	7	3	9	7	10	8	9
8	11	2	9	—	0	8	2	6	0	2	5	7	6
8	11	2	9	0	—	8	2	6	0	2	5	7	6
0	3	6	1	8	8	—	6	2	8	6	11	9	10
6	9	0	7	2	2	6	—	4	2	0	7	9	8
2	5	4	3	6	6	2	4	—	6	4	11	11	12
8	11	2	9	0	0	8	2	6	—	2	5	7	6
6	9	0	7	2	2	6	0	4	2	—	7	9	8
11	8	7	10	5	5	11	7	11	5	7	—	2	1
9	6	9	8	7	7	9	9	11	7	9	2	—	1
10	7	8	9	6	6	10	8	12	6	8	1	1	—

SELECTED REFERENCES

Bickford, E. Woody. 'Human Circadian Rhythms: A Review'. New York: Lighting Research Institute, 1988.

Buley, L.E. 'Experience with a Physiologically-based Formula for determining Rest Periods on Long-Distance Air Travel'. *Aerospace Medicine*, Vol. 41, Number 6, June 1970.

Carper, Jean. *The Food Pharmacy*. New York: Bantam Books, 1988.

Coleman, Richard M. *Wide Awake at 3.00 A.M.* New York: W.H. Freeman and Company, 1986.

Corfman, Eunice. *Depression, Manic-Depressive Illness, and Biological Rhythms*. Rockville, Maryland: National Institute of Mental Health, U.S. Department of Health and Human Services, 1979.

Czeisler, Charles A. *et al.* 'Bright Light Induction of Strong (Type O) Resetting of the Human Circadian Pacemaker'. *Science*, 16 June 1989, Vol. 244, 1328-1333.

Daan, Serge and Lewy, Alfred J. 'Scheduled Exposure to Daylight: A Potential Strategy to Reduce Jet Lag Following Transmeridian Flight'. *Psychopharmacology Bulletin*, Vol. 20, Number 3, 1984, 566-568.

Dryer, Bernard and Kaplan, Ellen S. *Inside Insomnia*. New York: Villard Books, 1986.

Finkelstein, Silvio. 'Rest can help Travellers after Long Flights'. *I.C.A.O. Bulletin*, International Civil Aviation Organization, November 1972.

Freedman, Daniel X. *et al.* 'Drugs and Insomnia'. *Consensus Development Conference Summary*, Vol. 4, Number 10. Washington, D.C.: National Institutes of Health, U.S. Department of Health and Human Services, 1983.

Hausman, Patricia and Hurley, Judith Benn. *The Healing Foods*. Emmaus, Pennsylvania: Rodale Press, 1989.

Lamberg, Lynne. *The AMA Guide to Better Sleep*. New York: Random House, 1984.

Luce, Gay Gaer. *Biological Rhythms in Psychiatry and Medicine*. Washington, D.C.: National Institute of Mental Health, U.S. Department of Health, Education and Welfare, 1970.

Lynch, H.J. *et al.* 'Daily Rhythms in Human Urinary Melatonin'. *Science*, January 17, 1975.

Lynch, H.J. *et al*. 'Melatonin Excretion of Man and Rats: Effect of Time of Day, Sleep, Pinealectomy and Food Consumption'. *International Journal of Biometeorology*, 19, No. 4, 1975.

McFarland, Ross A. 'Air Travel across Time Zones'. *American Scientist*, January-February 1975.

Minors, D.S. and Waterhouse, J.M. 'Circadian Rhythms and Aviation'. *Aviation Medicine Quarterly*, 1, 1987, 9-26.

Mohler, Stanley R. *et al*. 'The Time Zone and Circadian Rhythms in relation to Aircraft Occupants taking Long-Distance Flights'. *American Journal of Public Health*, August 1968.

Morgan, Brian L.G. and Morgan, Roberta. *Hormones*. Los Angeles, California: The Body Press, 1989.

National Institute of Mental Health. *Sleep Disorders*. Washington, D.C.: U.S. Department of Health and Human Services, 1987.

Palmer, John D. 'Biological Clocks of the Tidal Zone'. *Scientific American*, February 1975, 70-77.

Palmer, John D. *Introduction to Biological Rhythms*. New York: Academic Press, Inc., 1976.

Petrie, Keith *et al*. 'Effect of Melatonin on Jet Lag after Long Haul Flights'. *British Medical Journal*, 18 March 1989, Vol. 298, 705-707.

Raloff, Janet. 'Biological Clocks: How They Affect Your Health'. *Scientific Digest*, November 1975, 62-69.

Regestein, Quentin R. *Sound Sleep*. New York: Simon and Schuster, 1980.

Reppert, Steven M. *et al*. 'Putative Melatonin Receptors in a Human Biological Clock'. *Science*, 7 October 1988, Vol. 242, Number 4875, 78-81.

Rose, Kenneth Jon. *The Body in Time*. New York: John Wiley and Sons, Inc., 1988.

Saunders, David S. *An Introduction to Biological Rhythms*. New York: John Wiley and Sons, Inc., 1977.

Sobel, Michael I. *Light*. Chicago, Illinois: University of Chicago Press, 1987.

Still, Henry. *Of Time, Tides and Inner Clocks*. Harrisburg, Pennsylvania: Stackpole Books, 1972.

Thompson, Leonard J. 'Disorders of Circadian Rhythm with Air Travel'. *Patient Management*, December 1986, 13-20.

Ward, Ritchie R. *The Living Clocks*. New York: Alfred A. Knopf, 1971.

Weston, Lee. *Body Rhythm*. New York: Harcourt Brace Jovanovich, 1979.

Winfree, Arthur T. *The Timing of Biological Clocks*. New York: Scientific American Books, Inc., 1987.

Wurtman, Richard J. 'Effects of Light and Visual Stimuli on Endocrine Function'. *Neuroendocrinology*, 2, 1967.

Wurtman, Richard J. 'The Effects of Light on the Human Body'. *Scientific American*, July 1975.

Wurtman, Richard J., and Moskowitz, Michael A. 'The Pineal Organ'. *New England Journal of Medicine*, 296, June 9 and June 16, 1977.

INDEX